DEFEATING
DEPRESSION

Further praise for **Defeating Depression**

"*Defeating Depression* . . . will give everyone who reads it a new perspective on a disease that has long been seeped in misconceptions and contempt."

William D. Po, M.D.
Wright State University Boonscroft School of Medicine

"Stone offers a framework for addressing the multiple dimensions of depression. Persons dealing with depression, family members and friends, as well as clergy and other helping professionals can benefit from this book."

Teresa E. Snorton
Executive Director, Association for Clinical Pastoral Education

"*Defeating Depression: Real Help for You and Those You Love*, not only provides a vocabulary for our most intense emotions and feelings associated with depression, it deciphers the often mysterious return to vitality. The work has quickly become my most effective tool in helping the depressed, their loved ones and educating pastoral caregivers."

W. Kyle Fauntleroy
Naval Chaplains School

DEFEATING
DEPRESSION

Real Help
for You and
Those Who
Love You

Howard W. Stone

Augsburg Books

MINNEAPOLIS

Cover design: Laurie Ingram
Cover image: © Lew Robertson/Corbis. Used by permission.
Interior design: Michelle L. N. Cook

Library of Congress Cataloging-in-Publication Data

Stone, Howard W.
  Defeating depression : real help for you and those who love you / Howard W. Stone.
      p. cm.
Includes bibliographical references (p.   ).
ISBN 978-0-8066-9031-5 (alk. paper)
1. Depression, Mental—Religious aspects—Christianity. I. Title.
BV4910.34.S76 2007
616.85'2706—dc22   2007022468

Large-quantity purchases or custom editions of this book are available at a discount from the publisher. For more information, contact the sales department at Augsburg Fortress, Publishers, 1-800-328-4648, or write to: Sales Director, Augsburg Fortress, Publishers, Box 1209, Minneapolis, MN 55440-1209.

The paper used in this publication meets the minimum requirements of American National Standard for Information Sciences—Permanence of Paper for Printed Library Materials, ANSI Z329.48-1984.

Manufactured in the U.S.A.

11   10   09   08   07   2   3   4   5   6   7   8   9   10

Contents

Acknowledgments   vi

Part One—Is It Depression or Something Else?
Introduction   3
1. Are You Depressed?   12
2. Depression on the Rise   20
3. Faces of Depression   28
4. Masquerade: Depression and Other Maladies   41
5. Hope Is a Future Word   51

Part Two—The Four Faces of Depression: What You Can Do
6. Body and Brain: The Physical Face of Depression   64
7. Physical Remedies   75
8. Medical Remedies   86
9. What Do You Think? The Cognitive Face of Depression   98
10. Those Negative Thoughts Keep Running through My Head   108
11. Think Again: How to Transform Your Thinking   117
12. Journey of a Thousand Miles: The Behavioral Face of Depression   135
13. Doing What Needs to Be Done   145
14. Effective Action: If It Works, Do It!   158
15. Living with a Depressed Person: The Interpersonal Face of Depression 171
16. A Healing Network: What Family and Friends Can Do   176
17. Help for the Whole Family   187

Part Three—Help for Depression
18. How to Save a Life: Suicide Prevention   194
19. Desolations: Depression and Spirituality   202
20. The Healing Spirit: Values and Purpose Can Defeat Depression   212
21. Getting Help   220
22. Hope and Happiness for a Lifetime   233

Appendix A—The Zung Self-Rating Depression Scale   235
Appendix B—Suggested Readings and References   239
Index   243

Acknowledgments

Several people generously gave their time to read this manuscript and offer careful and thoughtful criticism. My sincere gratitude goes to Duane Bidwell, Joey Jeter, Ryan Fraser, Christine Po, William Po, and John Fiedler for their invaluable contributions to the manuscript as you see it. Finally, I want to express my deep gratitude to Karen Stone who gave many hours of her time to reviewing the text and making it more readable.

Many of the ideas presented in this book are drawn from my day-to-day practice of counseling. Consequently, the book contains elements of actual case histories. Because confidentiality is essential to counseling practice, all case descriptions have been altered with respect to names and other identifiers to preserve anonymity while not distorting the central reality of the experience described.

Part One

Is It Depression
or Something Else?

INTRODUCTION

How To Use This Book

IN THIS INTRODUCTION YOU WILL:

✓ Find answers to the questions: What is depression? What is not depression?
✓ Read about the author's own experience of depression.
✓ Understand that this self-help book can guide you to manage and triumph over depression.
✓ Discover that it is written both for someone who is depressed and for family and close friends of the depressed person.
✓ Scan a brief summary of the book's chapters so that you can decide where you want to begin reading.
✓ Learn how to use the TAKE ACTION and FOR THE FAMILY boxes that you will find in each chapter.

Are you blue? Do you feel low, unusually tired, or sad much of the time? Have you lost interest in activities you once enjoyed? Do you have a family member or close friend who is depressed?

Perhaps you are uncertain. Is it depression, or is it something else? Take Sophie, for example. She strides into the break room at work, pours a cup of high-test coffee, and exclaims to her coworkers: "This day is already a disaster. I got a speeding ticket on the way to work, my husband will be *furious* because it's my second one this month. Then I find out my secretary's called in sick, the window in my office is leaking, I'm coming down with a cold, *and* today's the day Mr. Boss-Man has decided to do my performance review! I'm so depressed, I think I'll just give up and go back home." Is Sophie really depressed? It seems unlikely. She has energy and a sharp wit. True, she is stressed, and most of us would feel a little low, anxious, or unwell in her situation. She tells her friends that she is depressed, but then adds a facetious tag line. This will pass.

Unlike Sophie, perhaps you, or someone you love, are truly depressed and looking for a few specific things you can do to send depression packing.

This book is for you.

This year, one out of ten adults in the United States will feel the misery of depression that saps our energy and drains our spirit. Occurrences of this affliction are increasing steadily, and have been for the last half-century.

"Major depression" is what this book is all about. It is a medical term for a lasting and deeply affecting condition, more than a passing feeling of sadness or malaise. Major depression is also known as *melancholy* or *melancholia* (this book uses all three terms interchangeably).

Depression has four faces: physiological, cognitive, behavioral, and interpersonal (in simpler terms: your body, thoughts, actions, and relationships). In this book, I will suggest ways for you to effectively address each of these aspects of depression. I will show you specific steps that you can take to diminish suffering and increase joy and satisfaction in life. You do not have to continue suffering from the effects of depression. *It is not your fault,* but *only you* can do something about it.

I have walked in your shoes.

Over thirty-five years have now passed since I sat in bed at some ungodly hour of a long, sleepless night with my journal in my lap. As my wife slept beside me, I penned the following words.

I am lost in an immense underground cavern with tangled, unending passageways. What distant light I could once see soon shrank to a glimmer and now is gone. Earlier I tried mightily to get out, to find the light of day again, but it is no longer possible and I no longer care. I'm very, very tired.

My hand moved almost automatically over the pages. I was little more than an observer. The "cavern" was vivid, our bedroom only a shadow. I wrote on:

I don't have energy to turn back, to find my way out. It would be futile anyway. I have no real hope for the direction I am going. There is no real reason to continue but I am afraid to stop; I might never move again.

I am very cold. My hands are numbed by the cold, scarred, and caked with blood from my falls on the dark uneven floor.

People (those who wish me well and those who don't) are irritants. They want something from me, or they want to do something for me (which I do not want). I shudder at a knock on the door, the sound of the telephone. I wish all of them would be gone. There is nothing I want to do. Nothing excites me.

God is absent. Perhaps God has more important things to do elsewhere.

Why should I go on? I see no light, no end, no way out. Ahead is a useless journey, exhausted step followed by exhausted step, leading deeper into the unknown. Why not throw myself on the ground and let numbed sleep peacefully overcome me? I blunder on.

When I wrote these lines I had been depressed for several months, and months of deep melancholy still lay ahead. As bad as it felt, it wasn't incapacitating; I continued to function in my job, socialized with friends, visited my in-laws, stayed married. But there was no joy in any of it. The images and the despair of that cavern dominated my inner world for a long time.

As a therapist, I had helped many depressed people find their way out of the depths. Now I saw depression from their side. Now I didn't just know that my counselees hurt; I also knew, at least to some extent, what their pain felt like.

Depression is not a forgettable experience. I cannot erase the memory of the deep sadness and soul-wrenching agony that can accompany depression. It hurts, but not like the sharp pain of slamming a door on your finger. To me, depression feels more like the sick feeling in your stomach when something terrible has happened—except that it lasts and lasts, day after day, and seems as if it will never end. It's unrelenting.

When you mash your finger, it swells up. You can show the bruise to your friends and get a little sympathy. The pain of depression is just as real, but it doesn't show. You may not get a lot of compassion. My wife cared; she knew I was struggling but she couldn't comprehend the extent of it. She was still in her twenties, a full-time graduate student and the mother of an elementary school child. She tiptoed around my moods but never (thank God!) entered the cavern with me.

I am fortunate. That was my one and only serious episode of major depression. But to this day, I occasionally sense melancholy at the door. Sometimes it knocks gently; other times it rattles, pushes, and clamors to get in. Then I picture it as a dark form with its shoulder to the door of my inner world, shoving with all its might.

Sometimes I just have a general out-of-sorts feeling. Maybe I'm irritable or unusually impatient. At other times the pain of my constant low-level arthritis gets to me and I start feeling sorry for myself. (Back when I was able to play racquetball or tennis, I would notice that I moved around the court a little slower.) I might feel unaccountably bored, and nothing—not my job, fishing trips, long walks with my wife, visits with my daughter and granddaughters, or even my hobby of antique radio collecting—can capture my interest.

Fortunately, I know that any of these signs can mean that depression is lurking. It's important to pay attention, stay alert, and refuse to let these feelings take over. It's also important to take action, and so I undertake one or two of the activities described in this book (see the TAKE ACTION steps listed in each chapter).

TAKE ACTION

Are you satisfied with your life?

Take the following quick quiz (Diener 1985) to gain a general sense of your happiness and satisfaction with life. Write a number from one to ten that indicates your agreement or disagreement with each statement, with ten meaning you agree completely and one not at all.

____ In most ways, my life is close to my ideal.
____ The conditions of my life are excellent.
____ I am completely satisfied with my life.
____ So far, I have gotten the important things I want in life.
____ If I could live my life over, I would change nothing.

____ Add up your total

If your total was:	You are:
30-35	Extremely satisfied, much above average
25-29	Very satisfied, above average
20-24	Somewhat satisfied, average for U.S. residents
15-19	Slightly dissatisfied, below average
10-14	Dissatisfied, clearly below average
5-9	Very dissatisfied, much below average

If you scored very low:

✓ You may need to readjust your goals. Are they realistic? Do they require perfection?
✓ You may be placing a negative frame on neutral events or situations.
✓ You may need to seek out more meaningful activities. Begin very small (for example, volunteer to read storybooks to a child in an inner city school).

If you scored above average but still feel depressed:

✓ Have a thorough physical examination if you have not already done so.
✓ Ask your doctor if you would benefit from antidepressant medications.
✓ Perhaps you are setting your mark too low. Are your life goals easy to satisfy, but not challenging enough to provide you with a sense of meaning and accomplishment?

FOR THE FAMILY

Here is the first FOR THE FAMILY suggestion:

Begin conversations with your family member or friend about depression. You can open with a question such as: "What is it like to be depressed?" or "Although I have had times in my life when I was blue for a short period of time, I know that is not the same as what you are experiencing. Tell me what you are going through in your depression."

Keep the conversation brief. Don't lecture or tell the person how he or she should feel. Merely try to understand what they are experiencing. *Be very curious.* If the person has trouble talking or telling you about the depression, don't force the issue. Tell them: "Maybe at some other time you will be able to tell me about it or write down what you are experiencing." Then let it go and return to it another day. The reason that this exercise is helpful is because everyone experiences depression differently. You will learn how your family member or friend is experiencing it. Your family member will also learn that you are concerned.

CHAPTER ONE

Are You Depressed?

IN THIS CHAPTER YOU WILL:

✓ Read a more detailed discussion of what is and is not depression.
✓ Understand why you should probably see a physician if you suspect that you are depressed.
✓ Take a quick test to find out if you or a family member is depressed.
✓ Read about the degrees of depression and the important differences between mild, moderate, and severe depression.
✓ Learn that, because depression has no single cause, it is usually fruitless to spend time searching for the precise reasons for this depression.

Do you, or does someone you care for, suffer from depression? It's important to know. If what you are experiencing is a temporary sadness brought on by a crisis in your life, you'll find reassurance in knowing that it will pass. If what looks like depression actually is the result of a physical illness, finding the cause could save your life. (See chapter 5.) Learning the nature and severity of your dark mood is the necessary first step toward defeating or preventing depression.

When Nathan's wife left him, he felt despondent. He hadn't wanted a divorce. Their only child moved with his ex-wife, Camilla, to a city nearly 1,200 miles away.

Camilla had always taken care of Nathan; she had cooked, cleaned, paid the bills, balanced the checkbook, and planned their vacations. Now he felt helpless and incompetent. He had no relatives within a thousand miles. Nathan's friends at work tried to be supportive, and members of his church had rallied around in the first weeks after the divorce. But there were no more parties at his house (that had been Camilla's specialty). He went fishing with his buddies a couple of times, but they made jokes about Camilla and about divorce in general. Nathan had trouble entering into their good-natured ribbing.

Nathan thought he would adjust as time went by, but he only felt worse. Four months after the divorce, he still found himself weeping when anything reminded him of her. He had trouble sleeping. He missed his wife terribly.

Was Nathan depressed? Perhaps not. Four months is not a very long time after the severing of such an important relationship. His grief was still quite fresh. He lacked a community to grieve with him; he shed his tears alone, at home, in his car, sometimes in the men's room. Nathan's responses to the loss of his marriage were normal, but because of his isolation, he was walking the ragged fringe of depression. He needed to make some lifestyle changes, find supportive relationships, and take on one or two healthful activities to protect himself from a serious, long-term depression.

People usually feel down and distressed after an important loss, such as the death of a spouse or loved one, divorce, disability, or other significant loss. It's normal. In fact, it would be abnormal *not* to respond with sadness or grief.

If this sounds like you, there is no particular reason to believe you have a major depression—not unless you have been down for an unusually long period of time and don't seem to be coming out of it. Read on for tips that can prevent your sadness from taking over your life.

Isn't/Is

Depression is *not discouragement* in a life filled with physical pain, tragedy, or oppression. It is not cynicism or outrage. It is not a short spell of feeling blue or a passing bout of deep sadness. Nearly all people go through times when they feel down.

Depression is not sin. It is *not* your fault. If you struggle with depression, you need skills to address it and work to control it; you do *not* need to take on a load of guilt. This perspective smooths the way for positive change because once you have learned how to handle depression, you can move forward to a more hopeful and productive future.

Depression is not necessarily feeling sad or low. Many people experience ebbs and flows in their moods: periods of high and low energy, times when they accomplish a great deal and times when they do little or nothing, procrastinate, or waste time. Life is not a sitcom with characters who are always upbeat, clever, and witty. You need to recognize and accept that you can have periods of low mood; most people do. The important thing is what you do about it.

Many people try to deny their despondent feelings. They may act strong and in control, upbeat all the time. They may refuse to acknowledge what is happening to them. Others may admit to feeling depressed, but beat up on themselves for feeling that way. They may see themselves as sick, lazy, good-for-nothing, losers, and worse; they expect their lives to be like the lives of those absurdly euphoric young adults in beer commercials on TV.

Depression (also called *melancholia* or *melancholy* in this book) is a unique disorder because it affects the total human organism—your body as well as your thinking, feeling, interpersonal relationships, and behaviors. It has an infinite number of possible causes and triggers. Because it is so complex, the steps that you take to overcome depression need to be tailored to your own specific circumstances.

When to See a Doctor

It is important to keep in mind that some of depression's symptoms are also character-istics of physical diseases. Several years ago, I knew a man who described low mood, exhaustion, weight loss, and marital strife. He had a history of depressive episodes, but the rapid weight loss and his general out-of-sorts feeling suggested that his problem might be something other than depression or marital strife. A physical examination revealed that he had cancer and needed immediate surgery. After his recovery, the depressive symptoms vanished. Not the marital strife, however. After several sessions of marriage counseling, he and his wife began to achieve a more mutually satisfying relationship.

Important point!	**If you have any symptoms of depression, you need to have a thorough medical examination and tell the doctor your symptoms. Most likely you do not have a physical illness, but you *must* check it out. If you feel too shy or embarrassed to talk about your depression, get someone to do it for you or write it down on a piece of paper and hand it to your doctor.**

Take This Quiz before Moving On

Here is a quick checklist that you can use to find out if you or your loved one has symp-toms of depression. It is very important to remember that this checklist is a preliminary screening test only. It is intended solely for the purpose of identifying the symptoms of depressive disorders, and not to provide a diagnosis for major depressive disorder. As such, it cannot replace a formal therapeutic or psychiatric evaluation.

Remember, only a physician or qualified mental health professional can make an accu-rate diagnosis for depression (or any other psychiatric disorder), after giving a complete evaluation, including a physical exam to rule out any medical illnesses or conditions.

The Quiz

Put a check mark in the box next to each of the following statements that refer to you and how you have felt, at least part of the time, for the last two weeks.

- [ ] Many mornings I wake up too early and have trouble going back to sleep.
- [ ] I have lost interest in things that I used to enjoy.
- [ ] I find that I am avoiding people.
- [ ] Many times it is an effort to leave the house.
- [ ] I find that I am increasingly irritated, even angry, over trivial things.
- [ ] I am tired a lot of the time and lack energy to do things I need to do.
- [ ] I am gaining or losing weight (more than 10 lbs. in the last 6 months or less if you are a female or small male).
- [ ] I feel as if I have lost control of my life.
- [ ] Most days of the week I feel blue, sad, or unhappy part of each day.
- [ ] My sleeping patterns have changed.
- [ ] Sometimes I think that people would be better off if I weren't around.
- [ ] I don't have the appetite that I use to have.
- [ ] I just can't seem to get things done like I used to do.
- [ ] I don't feel as happy as I used to feel.
- [ ] I feel guilty much of the time over things that never used to bother me.
- [ ] I often feel that I am not much good to anyone, including myself.
- [ ] I feel worse in the morning than at other times of the day.
- [ ] I am not thinking as clearly as I used to, and it is harder to concentrate.
- [ ] I feel that things always go wrong no matter what I do.
- [ ] I have been depressed in the past.

Now add up your check marks.

✓ 0-3: You are reading this book to help someone else, or to try to prevent a future episode of depression.

✓ 4-6: You may be on the borderline of depression. Keep reading, and start doing the action steps listed at the end of each chapter.

✓ 7-9: There is a good chance that you are depressed. Put into action the ideas discussed here. Consider getting a physical.

✓ 10-12: It's likely that depression has haunted you for some time. Change is not only possible but also likely, if you take action and follow through. Be sure to treat yourself with tenderness along the way. See your physician to determine if there are physical causes for the way you feel.

✓ 13-20: Unless other factors influenced your answers, you appear to be suffering from significant depression. Start working on the changes that are discussed here.

See a physician and/or a psychotherapist to help guide you in addressing your melancholy (turn to chapter 22 for guidelines on selecting a therapist).

Remember that this quiz only determines *symptoms* of depression. If your score is medium to high (7 or more), I recommend that you take a more sophisticated test and/or see a physician or a counselor to help determine if you really are depressed.

The Zung Scale is in Appendix A	**You can use several inventories to help determine the existence and extent of your depression. These include the Beck Depression Inventory (1967), the Zung Self-Rating Depression Scale (1965), the Raskin Rating Scale for Depression (1970), and the Hamilton Rating Scale (1969).**

Ultimately, you must be the judge. If you are not feeling your old self or doing the things you used to do, you may be struggling with depression. Or, at the very least, it is knocking at your door.

Is It Really Depression?

You don't have to call it depression, melancholia, or melancholy. (It is good to note that psychiatrists refer to melancholia as a specific type of atypical depression, a distinction beyond the scope of this book.) All three terms are used interchangeably in this book; *melancholic* refers to a person who suffers from depression. Name it the blues, if you prefer. Whatever the label, this malady is very different from the occasional low periods that people go through in the course of living. Psychiatrists use the term *major depression* to distinguish it from normal, passing sadness. Criteria for diagnosing major depression include the following nine symptoms:

❑ Low mood, sadness, and irritability for part of nearly every day

❑ Reduced pleasure or interest in daily activities

❑ Considerable weight loss or gain, or a change in appetite

❑ Significant change in sleeping patterns (most common is early waking)

❑ Marked increase or decrease in movement (usually a slowdown)

❑ Fatigue and loss of energy

❑ Feelings of worthlessness or guilt

❑ Difficulty concentrating

❑ Ideas about suicide or death

According to the American Psychiatric Association, a person who exhibits at least *five* of these symptoms for a minimum of two weeks and has either low mood or reduced pleasure/interest for at least part of most days suffers from major depression (APA 1994).

"Wait a minute," you might say. "Checking items off a list can't tell the whole story of my unique experience." You would be right, but these criteria serve as a good starting point for determining if depression exists. They signal a possible problem.

How Bad Is It?

Can you weigh the severity of your own depression? Yes, you can. The extent of a true depression is ranked as mild, moderate, or severe. You may find encouragement in learning that your condition is mild or moderate, but if your depression is severe, you need to know it so that you can get the help you need to pull out of it. By a vast majority, most individuals are only mildly depressed and will reap immense benefits by doing some of the exercises this book suggests.

The Different Levels of Depression

Mild

In mild depression, you may feel sad or blue. This feeling comes and goes; at times you may be quite cheerful. Possibly you lose interest in work or hobbies, suffer from insomnia, or experience moderate but uncharacteristic fatigue or restlessness. The unwell feeling can improve temporarily (or permanently) with compliments and jokes, a new job, a vacation, or a piece of good news. Other symptoms of mild depression may get better with regular, strenuous exercise, a reevaluation of goals, changes in diet, and similar measures.

Moderate

If moderately depressed, you tend to feel sadder and lower more of the time. You are less responsive to attempts at offering cheer. The low mood is usually worse in the morning and may lighten somewhat as the day progresses. Many people who are moderately depressed pull away from friends and family, and their relationships may be troubled.

Severe

It seems as if those who struggle with severe depression live on a dismal and barren planet. In severe depression, you are apt to feel relentlessly hopeless and miserable. Your sadness is painful. You feel hopeless. Often you slow down to an extreme, can't think clearly, and feel exhausted and passive. Your relationships and your normal functioning suffer greatly. Severe depression usually calls for therapy and medications.

No Single Cause

Let's not try to pinpoint the exact cause of a particular depression. It's not necessary. Probably it's impossible. There could be a genetic predisposition, previous occurrences of depression, worries or anger about social injustice, unrealistic expectations, distorted thinking styles, a troubled relationship, unhealthy diet or drug use, and many, many more causes.

Life is full of risk. When you apply for a job, you risk not getting it. When you bake a cake or paint a picture, you risk that others may not like it. When you love someone, you risk being rejected if your loved one leaves you or being left alone if your loved one dies.

It is not what happens to people that causes depression. Many get turned down for job after job without becoming depressed. Parents die, children get in trouble with the law, siblings commit suicide, spouses leave, houses burn down, businesses fail—and the wounded carry on. People have lost entire families in automobile accidents or natural disasters and yet, though their grief is unfathomable and will never leave them entirely, do not succumb to depression.

Why, then, do some people plummet into the depths of depression after a tirade from a stranger at an intersection? A perceived snub from a neighbor? A mixed performance review at work? It is completely normal to feel bad when bad things happen; getting depressed over them is a different matter entirely.

How we think about depression shapes how we will respond to it. First, it is a *disorder*, not a disease like cancer. There is no blood test for depression, no way it will show up on an MRI (magnetic resonance imaging). In fact, it may be better to talk about depressions, plural, because no single cause or symptom defines it.

Indeed, if you had a chance to look at videotapes of counseling with melancholic people, you would see many shapes and colors of depression. For some, melancholia mainly affects their personal relationships. Others experience dark emotions. Still others just stop doing what they used to do. Many people distort what is happening around them; they think about positive events as neutral, and neutral events as negative.

If you suffer from even mild depression, by now you have heard people urge you to cheer up. They may have told you that if you only try hard enough or want to change badly enough, you will change. Don't listen to them! Let me go on record from the beginning: *the wish to change is not enough*. It's very important, to be sure, but you also need to develop a specific plan and take appropriate steps to overcome your depressive symptoms.

You already have the desire to change your depression. How do I know? You picked up this book. It's a good beginning. In these pages you will find methods, tips, and tricks that you can use to develop a plan to control your melancholy, to conquer the effects of depression, and to move forward into a satisfying and hope-filled life.

TAKE ACTION

Take the quick checklist included earlier in this chapter. It allows you to find out if you have the typical symptoms of depression. This checklist is a preliminary screening test only, but can give you an idea if depression is troubling you. If you haven't taken the quiz yet, why not do it now?

FOR THE FAMILY

✓ Take the depression quiz provided in this chapter—twice.

✓ The first time, take the quiz for yourself. It is good to know if you are beginning to slip into depression because living with someone who is melancholic makes you especially vulnerable.

✓ The second time, answer the questions as if you were the family member about whom you are concerned. Try your best to be that person for five or ten minutes. Doing so may help you discern if depression is the real problem.

✓ Now spend some time in the family talking about the answers to your quizzes. Listen to how others think and feel. Begin talking about how the family can respond to the impact of the depression on the family.

CHAPTER TWO

Depression on the Rise

IN THIS CHAPTER YOU WILL:

✓ Learn that you are not alone; depression is occurring at epidemic proportions not only in North America, but throughout the world.
✓ Become aware that people are more vulnerable to an episode of depression if they have experienced depression in the past.
✓ Place depression in history.
✓ Find out what depression is and how it develops.
✓ Focus on what psychiatrists call *major depression,* something quite different from feeling blue for a few days or grieving a spouse's death.
✓ Discover that suffering from depression is not a sign that you are weak, morally deficient, or despicable.

Melancholy. Despair. Depression.
By Whatever Name, It Seems Like an Epidemic

Depression is on the rise. Perhaps as many as twenty million have some form of depression at any given moment (Yapko 1999, 16). Even as you read this book the numbers grow. During any given year, almost one out of ten adults in the United States has some significant depressive disturbance (Regier, Narrow, & Rae 1993). In a recent study only angina (heart pains) caused greater physical impairment than depression, but depression came out highest of all disorders in terms of days in hospital beds (Fawcett 1993).

Depression's growth is global; a study of inhabitants of Western Europe, North America, the Middle East, and Asia recorded striking increases (Dayringer 1995, xvi). The increase of depression in the United States is happening so fast that the reasons are hard to interpret.

Are more people really becoming depressed? Or are they simply more educated about mental health issues, less reticent to admit to their depressive symptoms, more willing to seek treatment? After all, today it is more socially acceptable to go to a therapist or minister with a mental health problem than it was several decades ago. Be that as it may, there is plenty of data (including studies conducted in a number of different countries) to demonstrate that a fast-growing percentage of people are becoming depressed. The incidence of depression has increased anywhere from *three to ten times* since the end of World War II.

Although melancholia is increasing steadily in all age groups, there is a noticeable shift toward younger people. Depression can start at any age, however, it now most commonly begins in one's twenties or thirties.

The earlier it begins, the more pain depression will cause over a lifetime. More than half of those who experience one bout of depression will undergo another. More than 70 percent of people who have suffered two melancholic episodes will have a third, and almost 90 percent of all who have had three episodes of depression will have another one or more. Some people's second or third spells of depression come after many years of normal, symptom-free living. For others, the depressive episodes occur with increasing frequency (U.S. Vol. I 1993, 21). Those who do not get some form of help (and they are the majority) can expect their depression to last somewhere between six and twenty-four months.

Since it strikes especially during the adult, career-building, child-rearing years, depression affects not only the individual but also the marriage, family, workplace, and community. It is the common cold of mental and emotional disorders.

Don't let that discourage you! Don't put this book down. Don't say, "What's the use, I'll probably have another episode anyway." *There is hope.* You can do something to combat your black mood; that's what this book is about. I will show you a number of small, doable steps you can take that will diminish the impact of depression and reduce the chances that you will be laid low by another episode.

It is to answers and solutions, not problems, that this book is devoted.

Is Depression a New Phenomenon?

Melancholia did not appear on the scene suddenly in modern times. You can find descriptions of depression and explanations for its causes throughout recorded history. In Shakespeare's *The Merchant of Venice*, Antonio complains (In Solomon, 2001, 29):

> *It wearies me, you say it wearies you;*
> *But how I caught it, found it, or came by it*
> *What stuff 'tis made of, whereof it is born*
> *I am to learn;*
> *And such a want-wit sadness makes of me,*
> *That I have much ado to know myself.*

The depressive experience is complicated, and there are many ways to view it. Mary Louise Bringle (1996, 331) cautions against oversimplifying depression:

> The biological reductionist says, "Can't you just give me a pill and make me well?" The spiritual reductionist says, "It must be God's will that I'm suffering, so I've got to figure out why I'm being punished." The sociopolitical reductionist concludes, "If only I weren't living in this oppressive society I wouldn't have so much to be depressed about," and the sociopsychological reductionist laments, "If only I weren't in this bad relationship playing out all the destructive scripts from bad relationships in my past, I wouldn't be so unhappy."

All of these responses have the ring of truth, but none captures the complexity of depression. Oversimplification is dangerous because it skips too many aspects of what people suffering with depression really experience.

That is one reason why, no matter how real the oppression of sexism, racism, ageism, and other forms of social injustice, no matter how awful the history of verbal, physical, or sexual abuse, no matter how heart-rending the tragic circumstances, *when dealing with depression the focus must be upon taking responsibility for one's own well-being* to the fullest extent possible.

Blaming something or someone else for one's melancholia is too easy, too one-dimensional, too conveniently grasped onto by those who may already have a victim mentality. It seldom leads to healing.

What Causes Depression?

Is depression caused by one's environment—that is, by one's upbringing, family, friends, or society? Or is it a matter of physiology, of biochemical imbalances, genes, and the like? There is no clear answer, unless the answer is "both." (chapter 6 will discuss this puzzler in more detail.)

Some people do seem to be more physiologically vulnerable to depression than others; in fact, depression is the most organically-based of emotional afflictions. But if depression has physical causes, shouldn't the sufferer be given antidepressants rather than taking on the changes advocated by this book?

Well, yes. And also, no. Research suggests that various forms of antidepressants are at least somewhat helpful for 75 percent of those who are depressed, but that leaves 25 percent who cannot be helped by drugs—those who are unwilling to take medication or who suffer from side effects that preclude their use. What's more, it is not a good idea to rely on medication alone. Even small lifestyle changes such as this book describes can produce relief regardless of whether one's depression is due to environment or physiology or some of both.

It's not your fault . . . but you can fix it!

This sounds like a contradiction of terms, doesn't it? Even so, it is true. Perhaps you've read other books on depression. Most of them stress that depression is not your fault. It's nobody's fault. You are not to blame. Depression is nothing to be ashamed of. It may be an illness, like diabetes, or a condition, such as poor circulation or crossed eyes. It may be genetic. Suffering from depression is not a sign that you are weak, morally deficient, or despicable.

This is extremely important to remember. You might want to tattoo it on your forehead, inscribe it above your doorway, write it in lipstick on your bathroom mirror, tape it on your dashboard: *NO ONE IS TO BLAME.*

Why is it so important to remember that depression is not your fault? That it's nobody's fault? Because one of the characteristics of depression is hopelessness. The more you blame yourself or others, and the more people admonish you to cheer up, get a grip, go out and buy a new hat, the deeper you sink into helplessness and melancholia. The more ashamed you feel, the less likely you are to ask for help.

When public figures openly discuss their struggles with depression, humorists may use it for laughs and cynics may question their motivation, but the result is positive and valuable. Openness about depression demystifies and deblames. It says, in ways more profound than I or any author can tell you: *Depression is not something to be ashamed of.*

FAMOUS PEOPLE WHO "CAME OUT" WITH THEIR DEPRESSION

Mike Wallace, news anchor/analyst	Barbara Bush, former first lady
William Styron, author	Germaine Greer, author and activist
Buzz Aldrin, astronaut	Cher, entertainer
Art Buchwald, writer and humorist	Yves Saint Laurent, designer
Dick Clark, TV host	Paul Simon, musician and composer
Roseanne Arnold, actor, comedian	Elton John, musician
John Kenneth Galbraith, economist	Rodney Dangerfield, comedian
Stephen Hawking, physicist	Harrison Ford, actor
Dick Cavett, TV personality	Dolly Parton, musician
Michael Crichton, author	Monica Seles, pro tennis player
John Cleese, actor	Lionel Aldridge, football player
Carrie Fisher, actor	Boris Yeltsin, former Russian
Ted Turner, media mogul	president

CHAPTER THREE

Faces of Depression

IN THIS CHAPTER YOU WILL:

✓ Stop to think about an important fact that may surprise you: Depression may seem like it's all about feelings, but unfortunately our emotions can be unreliable sources of information and understanding.

✓ Organize your thinking about the causes and signs of depression, which fall into four categories: physiological (your body), cognitive (your thinking), behavioral (what you do), and interpersonal (your relationships).

✓ Learn about the relationship between gender and depression, and why women are almost twice as likely to become depressed as men.

✓ Find spiritual comfort in knowing that it is not at all unusual for depressed individuals to experience a certain deadness or dryness in their spiritual life.

What Is It Like to Be You?

You are like a snowflake; no one else is exactly the same as you. Some people's central experiences of melancholia may only be side issues for you, and vice versa. To overcome depression, first you need to learn those unique ways in which you experience low times in your life. Then you will able to focus on your own personal key issues and progress along your personal main roads without becoming lost in a warren of side streets.

No one else's experience of melancholia is exactly like yours—but you are not the only one who suffers these feelings. Think of a time when you read an article or watched a TV program about someone who suffers from depression. Perhaps you said to yourself, "Yes! That's me! I do that!"

You are unique, but not strange. People who struggle with depression report a number of similar symptoms. It is very unlikely that a single person would exhibit all of them. One may be exhausted all the time and have trouble talking to people, yet have no sleep disturbance. Another may experience immense sadness and a loss of satisfaction in what before had been pleasing activities, but few other signs of depression.

The Problem with Feelings

Depression can seem like it's all about feelings, can't it? Often you feel bad. Sometimes you feel good, but you don't notice it or you don't trust it. Other times you may feel nothing at all.

Feeling bad

Sometimes depression hurts. It may hurt physically. You might experience unbearable headaches, unexplained physical ailments, sore joints and muscles, nausea, cramps, stomachaches, and the like.

It may hurt emotionally. Perhaps you feel sad all the time, cry for little or no reason, hate yourself, feel lonely and alienated from friends and family, fear things that didn't use to frighten you. You may experience panic attacks, suspicion, resentment, anger, or a kind of free-floating, heart-rending grief.

Feeling nothing

Sometimes depression is like anesthesia. You are numb. You don't feel especially sad; in fact, you're not sure you feel anything at all. Nothing infuriates you, but nothing excites you either. You feel little love for people whom you should love. Movies, travel, get-togethers, celebrations don't interest you—you'd rather stay home. You expect little from life, and get less.

Perhaps you would rather not feel. Maybe "feeling" has meant "feeling pain" for so long that (consciously or unconsciously) you now prefer to deaden the nerve endings of your emotions. It seems safer. But feeling pain is being alive. You may shrink from it, but *everyone* feels it.

Everyone, you say? You look around, and you see people who appear blessed. All of their loved ones are still alive. They have enough money. They smile. They have good jobs. They go out in the world and function. They seem confident and happy.

Never forget: These people also feel pain. They have felt unloved, unworthy, and unattractive. They have experienced physical pain, anger, rejection, failure, and alienation. What is different between these people and you?

Okay, maybe they have more money, but not necessarily. They may have been lucky enough to choose a partner who would be loyal and loving throughout a lifetime. Or they're divorced and moving on. They may have natural abilities that help them move through life easily, but it's just as likely that you are equally intelligent and gifted.

Why aren't these people stuck in a mire of low feelings? It is possible they are not genetically predisposed to depression. It is possible that, at the present, things are going better for them. It is possible that they simply accept pain as a natural part of living, don't dwell on it, and face the future with hope.

Sex drive

Melancholia can bring a diminished appetite for sex; the severely depressed may lose their libido entirely and view sex as an intrusion into their private world.

Sleep problems

Do you lie awake in the wee hours of the morning? Sleep disturbances plague many depressed individuals. Insomnia is widespread, especially waking early in the morning and being unable to get back to sleep. Early morning waking is by far the number one sleep difficulty that can plague the depressed. It is so commonplace, in fact, that everyone evaluating symptoms of depression needs to ask, "Have my sleep patterns changed? Do I wake up early and have trouble getting back to sleep?"

A few depressives get more sleep than normal—as much as fourteen to sixteen hours or more each day, though often not at usual bedtimes. I have known people who would fall asleep at one or two in the morning, wake up just long enough to get their children off to school, and then sleep again until moments before the children arrived home.

Thinking: The Cognitive Face of Depression

I have pointed out that trusting your negative emotions can be dangerous. Unfortunately for the depressed, during your low times you also may not be able to trust your thoughts. Depression affects people's thinking; they tend to distort and misinterpret reality. It's often said that your perception is your reality. Depressed individuals have distorted perceptions of all that is around them—and those distortions are usually negative.

Events

Melancholics interpret everything that happens to them or around them in terms of defeat, threat, abandonment, and deprivation. For Margo, if a friend didn't answer the telephone, it meant she was avoiding Margo's call and rejecting her friendship. When her dog died of old age, God was punishing and abandoning her. When Margo got stuck in traffic on her way to an office gathering, she just knew that everyone would be furious at her, would say bad things about her, and would never invite her back. She saw neutral or even positive transactions with other people as disaster.

Self

Depressed individuals often view their own selves as useless, miserable, unlucky, unlikable, or helpless. When compared to others, they find themselves wanting. They commonly indulge in self-blame and self-criticism. Often they magnify their mistakes—as in the case of Rudy, who inadvertently offended a customer, then promptly marched into his boss's office and tendered his resignation. Feelings of guilt hang over them like a cloud.

Future

People suffering from melancholia can view the future as a continuation of everything bad from the past and the present. Or they can't see the future at all. Often they find it hard to concentrate. They may be indecisive, spending immense amounts of time trying to make a choice, looking for the perfect solution or the only right path. They focus primarily on the past. They suffer hopelessness, view a negative future of ongoing suffering and pain, feel trapped. To them, time most emphatically does not heal all wounds.

Instead of recognizing the specifics in a context ("Julie didn't answer the phone; she must be out shopping," "My dog died at the age of fourteen; I miss him, but that's a pretty long time for a dog to live," "I made a bad judgment call and lost a customer, but I can learn from my mistake and do better next time"), they sometimes think globally (Julie is not out shopping; she's screening her calls and doesn't want to talk to me.) When mixed with blaming and a negative distortion of reality, global thinking can cause melancholics to spend many waking hours musing over dreadful possibilities (see chapters 9 to 11).

Such negative thinking often begins when people have bad experiences over which they have no control. In a surprisingly short period of time, they quit trying to improve their situation. Assuming they will fail, they abandon hope. Viewing a goal as daunting or overwhelming, and unable to see any small, achievable steps toward realizing their objective, they turn away from it.

This concept was played out in a trivial but telling way when we lived in Arizona and our daughter, Christine, was in the sixth grade. We backed our car out of the garage for a short trip to visit grandparents in California; Christine's task was to pull down and lock the garage door. As we watched from the car, she looked up at the cord, which had broken and was hanging about ten inches above her reach. She stopped, turned, and gave us a beseeching look. At this point it would have been easy for one of us to jump out of the car, say, "Oh, honey, it's too high for you," and do it for her. Instead, we sat and smiled at her. I raised my hands toward her, palms up, as if to say, "Go for it!"

Christine's first response was exasperation, but seeing that we made no move to help, she found something to stand on and lowered the door herself. Task accomplished, she bounced into the car confidently, displaying not a shred of the helplessness and irritation that we had seen on her face only moments before.

Religion

In my personal and clinical experience, those who struggle with depression perceive God and religion in the same negative and hopeless manner. Although religion is not based on cognition alone, the depressed sometimes are especially troubled by doubts or even lose their faith entirely. They have trouble saying with the Psalmist, "My hope is in the Lord." A steadfast faith that could not be pried loose by untold earlier adversities, even tragedies, may crumble under the weight of depression.

Negativity

When Tyrone was driving on the Interstate, a bird flew into the grille of his car. The first words out of his mouth were: "Oh no, my radiator is destroyed!" When his boss retired, Tyrone told everyone who would listen that he was going to lose his job. His wife announced she was going to visit her sister for two weeks, and Tyrone wept. "I've known for quite a while that you aren't in love with me anymore. You want to get away from me, and I don't blame you. I make your life miserable."

Melancholics like Tyrone tend to view themselves, events, and the future negatively (Beck 1979). This negative perspective stretches its fingers into relationships, exaggerating the bad and overlooking the good.

Less to give

The depressed also have reduced psychic and physical energy, and therefore have less to give in relationships. They're unable to perform many of the little nurturing acts that people offer one another—smiles, phone calls, greetings, thoughtful comments. They might fly off the handle at people around them, sometimes suddenly, without an obvious reason.

People who are irritable, neglectful, and negative are less than desirable companions. Those who lack patience and understanding may shun the depressed, either because they don't get it or because they are uncomfortable and don't know how to offer help.

Dependency

Some depressed individuals become extremely dependent. Feeling helpless and hopeless, they are more likely to rely upon others for what they believe they are unable to provide themselves.

Joanna, for example, refused to leave the house and spent most of her time in bed or sitting in a well-worn recliner. Her daughter brought in meals, cleaned her house, arranged for lawn mowing and snow shoveling, and paid her bills. By the time the family sought outside help, Joanna had stopped taking care of her own personal hygiene; the only task she continued doing for herself was going to the toilet.

Withdrawal

Others who struggle with depression undergo a loss of emotional attachments—both the desire to associate with others and, because they have withdrawn from people, the actual opportunity to be in relationships. Take Rowena, who screened all telephone calls, only answering telemarketers and never people she knew. She shunned invitations. If she recognized someone coming toward her on the sidewalk, she would quickly cross to the other side of the street. Before she stopped going to church altogether, she would sit in the back pew and hurry out at the end of the service.

Melancholics who do interact with people tend to have interpersonal problems. They may not express their feelings to others in a responsible way. They may find it hard to assert themselves or, at the other extreme, may erupt easily in destructive rage.

For a somewhat extreme example, when Junior was depressed he would shake his fist, curse, and occasionally flip his middle finger at other drivers if they went too fast or too slow, stopped at a yellow light or went through a yellow light, talked on their cell phones, or drifted into his lane. He broke an automated teller machine when it ate his credit card. At home, he smashed a dish when he found dried egg on it, kicked a hole in a door that was stuck after a rain, and yelled at his children when they were too noisy.

Family problems

It is often hard to determine whether depression causes family difficulties or vice-versa. We do know that depressive episodes are more likely to occur after significant marital conflict, and that people are especially prone to depression following the end of an important relationship.

Abandoned by his wife when she tired of his gloomy outlook, Ralph fell into an even deeper pit of downheartedness and could not find a way out of it. He developed a multitude of physical ailments, some real and some imagined. Eventually, Ralph died of a twisted bowel (though he told his brother it was his heart that was broken).

Several research studies show that problems in marriage or family relationships tend to precede periods of depression (Ilfeld 1977; Beach & Nelson 1990). More research will help to shed light on this chicken-egg question, but one thing is clear: people with marriage problems are more likely to have melancholic symptoms than those who have fairly smooth-functioning marriages. If a woman views her relationship with her husband as unsatisfactory, she has as much as a one in two chance of being depressed (Beach et al. 1990; Weissman 1985).

Impact on children

Depression in parents can have a serious effect on children, and many children who have problems in school or are brought for counseling are found to have a parent who is suffering from melancholia. Several research studies that directly observed parent-child interactions suggest that depressed parents are less responsive to their children and less able to resolve parent-child conflicts (Field, Healy, Goldstein, & Guthertz 1990; Gordon et al. 1989; Radke-Yarrow, Nottlemann, Belmont, & Welsh 1993).

FOR THE FAMILY

Don't wait to be asked; seek as much knowledge as time allows.

✓ Assess the four characteristics of depression described in this chapter: body, thinking, doing, and relating. Which ones affect your loved one most? In what ways? What effect do they have on the family? On you? You might get your own journal and write out your answers.

✓ Gather information on depression. Contact some of the resources listed in chapter 22. Look on the Web, call 800 numbers, or talk to an organization such as your local mental health association. Take notes.

✓ Generate a list of helpers that you or the depressed person (or both) could engage if needed. Have the list ready in case the need arises or your loved one suddenly becomes willing to seek outside help. See chapter 22 for hints on how to find a good helper (minister, therapist, psychiatrist).

✓ Place helpful books, articles, or tapes about depression around the house for the depressed person (when motivated) to pick up and use. Many people who are suffering from depression do not want to read about it, but a window of openness or curiosity may open up when you least expect it. Therefore it is important to keep resources on hand (see the list of helpful books and articles in Appendix B).

CHAPTER FOUR

Masquerade: Depression and Other Maladies

IN THIS CHAPTER YOU WILL:

✓ Understand what other conditions often occur hand-in-hand with depression.
✓ Learn more about alcohol and depression.

Veronica didn't think of herself as being depressed. To her, depression seemed too much like mental illness, and she knew she wasn't mentally ill.

But Veronica also knew something wasn't right. She slept little at night but often dozed off at work. She was an intelligent woman (her grandfather used to call her a "smart cookie"), but now her mind seemed foggy. Whenever anything went wrong—even those day-to-day mishaps like dropping an egg on the floor or running out of gas—Veronica just froze; she couldn't think what to do.

Was Veronica depressed? Sometimes depression occurs hand-in-hand with other conditions. Let's look at several disorders that relate to—or can masquerade as—depression.

Anxiety

You have an uneasy mind. There are butterflies in your stomach all the time. Your palms sweat, your heart races, your head pounds, your shoulders ache, your knees wobble. Or you can't concentrate. You might breathe hard, talk more, talk less. Perhaps you suffer from ulcers, colitis, or indigestion. You flit from task to task or do nothing at all. These are physical symptoms of anxiety.

What is anxiety? It's a lot like fear. You perceive a threat of some kind—a threat of failure, threat of embarrassment, threat of losing your job, or some unknown free-floating threat that you can't quite name. You're not confident of your ability to handle the peril. Maybe you don't know where the threat is coming from, or when.

When your cave-dwelling ancestors encountered the very real threat of, say, an attacking tiger, adrenaline flowed in their veins and they either fled or fought the beast. You've got adrenaline in your blood, all right, but there's no animal to fight and nowhere to run. You're just apprehensive. You might also be depressed.

About 25 percent of depressed persons have high anxiety sometime during their depression. Panic attacks—sudden, intense spells of fear—are experienced by 10 to 20 percent. They may scream, run, hide, or shake violently. Their feeling of terror is real (U.S. Vol. I 1993, 47).

Depression can lead to anxiety, or vice versa. The longer people are anxious, the more likely they are to be depressed as well. In fact, some researchers consider anxiety and depression to be a single disorder, two sides of the same coin (Ibid., 48). Furthermore, some antidepressant medications can bring symptoms of anxiety as a side effect. Other antidepressants ease anxiety (see chapter 9 for a discussion of these medications).

Your doctor is on your side	*If you suffer from anxiety:* Talk to your doctor about it. If necessary, bring along a family member or close friend who can speak for you. If you are taking antidepressant medication and also experience generalized anxiety, panic attacks, or fear of going out in public, *it is critical that you tell your doctor about these feelings.* There are medications that can address both problems at the same time.

Eating Disorders

People who are troubled by an eating disorder are more likely to have or develop depression. The good news, for many, is that the medication they take for depression often helps them with their eating disorder. One woman who had been troubled by bulimia for years reported, "After I started taking Prozac, the urge to purge shrank to where I was able to control it and finally stop bingeing and purging for good."

Eating is necessary and important. It supplies energy, nutrition, camaraderie, aesthetic pleasure, and enjoyment in our lives. When eating takes over and becomes the goal in itself (not the nutrition, camaraderie, etc.), it becomes a problem.

People with an eating disorder are obsessed with food. They may come home from work intending to do a list of chores in the evening, but instead begin to eat—and soon the evening is gone. They may reject invitations to social engagements, and instead stay home and eat. They feel bad about eating, which makes them want to eat more. It's a vicious circle that mirrors depression itself.

Overeating/overweight

There are three primary forms of eating disorders. Surprisingly, the most common eating disorder *by far* is overeating—not anorexia or bulimia. Its principal symptom is obesity.

In fact, as the surgeon general recently announced, far more people damage their health and suffer from a variety of ailments such as diabetes, heart disease, stroke, and even cancer because of overweight than do all of the bulimics and anorexics put together. Overeating and overweight, it now appears, may cause more health problems and early death than smoking.

Anorexia nervosa

You see them on the cover of *People* magazine: skeletal celebrities, looking remarkably like famine victims with expensive haircuts and glitzy clothes. People who starve themselves (sometimes to death) are not ascetics. Their self-denial is not a spiritual discipline. Actually, anorexia is a form of food obsession. Its sufferers may not eat much of anything, but often they'll cook huge meals for others, plan elaborate menus, pore over cookbooks, and occasionally binge and purge.

Bulimia

In some ways bulimia is similar to anorexia. Both involve an obsession with food. Both can cause health problems. However, bulimics tend to binge on the foods they crave, followed by purging, which takes the form of excessive exercise, vomiting, taking large doses of laxatives, or subjecting themselves to a period of severe under-eating. Their weight tends to fluctuate, but usually is in the normal range.

Eating disorders and depression

Eating disorders often dovetail with depression because they allow people to:

- ✓ avoid the present
- ✓ shun responsibility
- ✓ turn a blind eye to reality
- ✓ procrastinate tasks
- ✓ believe their negative thoughts
- ✓ isolate from other people.

People with eating disorders are not always depressed, but an obsession with food certainly can make it much harder to manage depression.

> **If you have an eating disorder along with symptoms of depression:** I strongly recommend that you attend meetings of Overeaters Anonymous, a program based on the principles of Alcoholics Anonymous (www.overeatersanonymous.org). If you feel the need, see a therapist who will help you develop strategies for conquering your eating disorder as well as your depression. If eating makes you hungrier, consider eliminating sugar, starches, and alcohol from your diet, as these foods trigger the release of insulin into your bloodstream, thus lowering blood sugar and creating a feeling of insatiable hunger (Agatston 2003, xx).

See chapter 21

Obsessive-Compulsive Disorders

One of the most characteristic activities of depression is thinking obsessively about events of the past. People with obsessive-compulsive disorders (OCD) are even more likely to be depressed than those with eating disorders.

Jack Nicholson won an Academy Award for his portrayal of a person with OCD in the film *As Good As It Gets*. His character, Melvin Udall, never steps on a sidewalk crack, brings his own tableware to the café where he eats breakfast, and can't tolerate change in his rigid routine. Gradually we learn that Melvin is not such a mean-spirited man after all, but a sufferer with hope for a better future.

This is sometimes called "the doubting disease" because people with OCD doubt themselves, doubt that things are all right, fret about germs, and worry ceaselessly about just about anything.

Vicki was one of those doubters. She constantly worried that she might run out of toilet paper. Her linen closet was full of toilet paper. The cabinet under the sink bulged with toilet paper. She had toilet paper in the attic and toilet paper under the bed. In spite of this abundance, whenever Vicki went shopping, she doubted whether she had an adequate supply of toilet paper at home. Inevitably, she bought another sixteen-pack.

Obsessive-compulsive disorder may be just another face of depression. Many of the medications authorized by the U.S. Food and Drug Administration for the treatment of depression also help people troubled by obsessive-compulsiveness.

> **If you suspect you have obsessive-compulsive disorder and/or depression:** See your primary care physician for a checkup and discuss it with him or her.

If you are afraid to talk openly about your weird urges and obsessions, write them on a note card and hand it to the doctor, or bring along a friend to speak on your behalf. Do the exercises in this book, especially those in chapter 12. Once you know there is an alternative, you are not permanently trapped in your obsessions and compulsions.

Grief

Grief is not depression—though a grieving individual will usually experience depressive symptoms for a period of time. However, inadequate resolution of grief on some occasions can bring on depression.

Grieving people frequently describe bouts of depression-like symptoms that come and go with decreasing intensity and frequency after a loss. The grieving who also suffer from melancholia, however, find little relief from their pain. It goes on for months, or even years.

Do expect to return to normal functioning and a relatively level mood within a year or so. You will occasionally feel sad and miss the person for the rest of your life. But if you are not taking care of your personal needs, if you are avoiding social contacts, if your loss occupies your mind for a sizable portion of each day, you need to consider the possibility that you are suffering from depression and need to take action.

If you are grieving: **You are at risk for depression. Share your feelings with a close friend, minister, doctor, or psychotherapist. The depth of your love will not end simply because your loved one has died. It just changes.**

Read every paragraph of this book and do the exercises. Ask yourself: would my loved one have wanted me to spend the rest of my life grieving? Or would he/she want me to redirect the energy I once gave to our wonderful relationship toward some other person or task or cause that can benefit from my love?

Medical Disorders

I haven't forgotten Veronica! When she walked into my office and started listing her symptoms, I asked her if there was more she hadn't told me. She said, "Of course I'm totally exhausted all the time. I'm even tired after I've had a good sleep."

Anything else? Any aches and pains, headaches and such? "Well . . ." Veronica thought for a moment, "my shoulders ache a lot, like I've slept on them wrong or spent too much time at the computer."

Alcohol and Depression

Not everyone who drinks is headed for depression, and not every person struggling with melancholy uses alcohol. The fact remains, however, that alcohol is a depressant, and the melancholic who uses it is taking a life-threatening risk. *Alcohol seems to accelerate the downward spiral.*

Author John Hassler portrays to a T this whirlpool of alcohol-enhanced depression in *A Green Journey* (1985, 103–104). Randy moved on to a job selling water softeners and did all right until the sheer meaninglessness of water softeners overtook him. Faced with dismissal by the end of the week, Randy had a stroke of luck. He sold a deluxe model (earning him a commission of $140) to an attractive single woman who was new in town. His wife Janet was away in Ireland so he drove to a roadhouse, The Brass Fox, to celebrate:

> . . . where he sat at a wobbly little table and ordered a beer and a hamburger. The sale had excited him, and so had the buyer. He wondered why he hadn't stayed for dinner. Because he was married, that's why: one thing often led to another. But why (he asked himself halfway through his second beer), why, if he was all that firmly married, had his wife flown halfway around the world without him? . . . she truly needed to be away because Randy was such a glum husband. Yes, and he was worse than that—he was a heel. If he wasn't a heel he would have gone with her—she had begged him to go. Poor Janet. She deserved a better husband. He was moody and irritating and probably dull as dishwater. He drank his third beer and ordered a fourth.
>
> He'd be better, damn it, he'd change . . . Randy ordered his fifth beer. He liked beer. Beer lowered his spirits. He had come dangerously close to being happy this evening.

People who are already struggling with depression often have learned not to trust happiness. Alcohol cooperates by relieving some tension in the short term and then bringing them low. It affects the central nervous system and seems to increase the likelihood of depression.

Workers at alcohol rehabilitation centers report that the majority of alcohol abusing individuals who are depressed see their symptoms lift within a matter of weeks after they stop drinking.

Does excessive drinking cause depression, or does depression cause the misuse of alcohol? This is yet another chicken-egg question for which there is no clear answer. Certainly the two are associated. In an evaluation of twenty-four studies on alcoholism and depression, it was discovered that between 10 and 30 percent of alcoholics also experience depression at the time of evaluation (U.S. Vol. I 1993, 45). Some people who suffer from depression self-medicate themselves with alcohol.

You face a serious challenge in assessing your own drinking because many (or most) problem drinkers deny there is a problem. One of your first tasks as a depressed person who is drinking excessively will be to face your difficulties openly. Even light or occasional drinkers who are depressed need to consider foregoing alcohol altogether until the depressive episode has passed. For the depressed who are abusing alcohol, permanent abstinence is essential.

Online resources	*If your drinking is causing you problems at home or on the job, or if you or others are concerned about how much you drink:* It is worthwhile to do an assessment of alcohol use. You can contact any local alcohol and drug information center to help you make an assessment. You can use one of the self-assessment questionnaires on the Web, for example, www.health.org/gov-pubs/workit/efs2.aspx or www.caron.org/drug_alcohol_assess.asp. Or you can check out the Alcoholics Anonymous Website at www.alcoholics-anonymous.org.

If you take only one morsel from this chapter, let it be the importance of seeing a physician about your (or your loved one's) troubles. It is absolutely vital, if you suffer from the symptoms of depression, to find out whether your dark mood is really depression, or a physical illness masquerading as depression. Knowledge is power. Knowledge can save your life.

TAKE ACTION

What is the effect of circumstances such as health issues or bereavement on your low mood?

✓ Add more detailed notes about your situation and health to your journal entry in response to "What is it like to be you?" from chapter 3's TAKE ACTION box.

✓ Have you experienced grief, a heart attack or illness, problems with alcohol, or compulsive behaviors such as eating, shopping, or gambling? How have these circumstances affected your depression?

✓ Do an inventory of physical maladies. Does something in your body hurt, tingle, or feel numb? Are you forgetting more or falling down inexplicably? Do you notice changes in your vision? If so, keep a daily log of symptoms with time and details (upon rising, immediately after lunch, while walking, etc.).

✓ If you have even the slightest question about your physical condition, consult with your family physician. Put down this book and call for an appointment. Now.

FOR THE FAMILY

Many circumstances and medical conditions can masquerade as depression—some temporary or easily treated, others serious or even life-threatening.

✓ Convince your loved one to have a thorough medical examination. If possible, go along. Tell the doctor the symptoms you have noticed (or write them down on a piece of paper and give them to the doctor). It is important to rule out physical illness. Talk with the physician about the effect that other medical conditions can have on a person's mood. The doctor will also determine if any medications are in order.

✓ What if your loved one won't go to the doctor? *Don't nag.* When one approach doesn't work, abandon it immediately and try another. For example, if you share a primary care physician or practice, schedule concurrent or back-to-back annual physical exams, even if it's been less than a year since your last one. Or ask the person, in the nicest possible way, to "Do this for me."

✓ Has the person (or family) suffered a significant loss? Talk with your rabbi or pastor about the impact of grief on a person's mood. See a therapist if needed to sort out what is grief and what is depression (see chapter 22).

✓ If your family member is having trouble with drinking or an eating disorder, consider recommending a 12-step program like Overeaters Anonymous or Alcoholics Anonymous. Alanon or Alateen are similar organizations for family members of people who are having problems with alcohol. Check out the Alcoholics Anonymous Website at www.alcoholics-anonymous.org.

✓ To assist a family member who is depressed, you need support and help for yourself. Getting that help and support will make you better able to help your depressed family member.

CHAPTER FIVE

Hope Is a Future Word

IN THIS CHAPTER YOU WILL:

✓ Reflect that each of us lives in three time zones: the past, the present, and the future.
✓ Discover the importance of *projection*.
✓ Learn the benefits of *reframing*.

"Hope floats."—John Irving

When you hope, you sense that your troubles can end or become manageable.
When you hope, you recognize the possibilities that lie ahead.
When you hope, you invest energy in an exciting, promising future.

Past, Pesent, Future

We all live in three time zones: the past, the present, and the future.

The past is our given. No one can change it. It encloses our environment and upbringing, our culture, our bodies, our genetic makeup, personality, good and bad memories, and choices we have made.

The present is where we act. Here and now we exercise freedom within the limits of our situation, abilities, and past choices. (In spite of what some lucky, successful people might tell you, we cannot necessarily become whatever we want to be, not even "if we try hard enough.") We make choices and act freely, but we do so from the range of options available to us.

The future is all possibility. It is what we can become as we use our freedom. We are not robots. Our possibilities are not predetermined. We can imagine and, within the givens of life, can become something new. We anticipate the future with the awareness that we are free—however limited—to become who we ought to become. We take responsibility for shaping that future.

Melancholics allow their unhappy past to limit and dominate their future possibility by not taking new action in the present. The real anguish of depression comes not only from a negative past, but also from the loss of a positive future.

Unfortunately, many depressed persons spend a lot of energy focusing on the unhappy past. This is a grave error. If you are depressed, you need to sense hope—recognizing your givens from the past, to be sure, but also stepping directly into the future.

How do you step into the future? By exercising your freedom—that is, by taking action. Now.

There is good news! A number of simple methods and skills can create future hope—even when you are feeling depressed. Below you will find a listing of things you can do, beginning now, to start making make a positive, hoped-filled future.

The Future

A few years ago, with our daughter and her family, we visited the handsome Alpine city of Bolzano, where the Museum of Archaeology displays the oldest mummified body ever discovered. Oetzi (named for the Oetz valley in which he was found) was still wearing his leggings, tunic, and a woven grass cape when hikers came across his body in 1991. About 5,300 years ago, this forty-five-year-old man was traversing the Alps on foot when (recent DNA testing has revealed) he apparently encountered enemies and fell in a bloody struggle. Almost certainly a sudden blizzard covered him with ice and snow that remained for thousands of years, preserving his body almost perfectly. It was fascinating to gaze on him pretty much as he fell.

I tell this story because I'd like you to imagine what it's like to be stuck in time. Close your eyes and picture yourself frozen like Oetzi (but not dead). There will be no more change in your life and you will not alter in any way. You won't talk with anyone, you won't be influenced by anyone or anything, and you certainly won't watch TV or read books and magazines. Now open your eyes.

Could you do it? You will see at once that it is impossible not to change. Influences constantly press on us—what we read, what we see on television, our work, activities, friends and family.

In spite of evidence to the contrary, depressed individuals often think that they are frozen in time, like Oetzi. They are sure that the bad experiences of the past are destined to repeat into infinity. They see no possibility for a good or hopeful future.

They're mistaken. Even a hermit in the Northwest Territories of Canada, trapping and hunting his food and cutting logs for his shelter, can't avoid change. That hermit must respond to animals, food supply, blue or angry skies, rain, snow, drought, and his own aging body. Thus he is subject to change and even insight, growth, and improvement.

There aren't many hermits in the wilderness. Most of us have jobs, are accountable, take care of people, and as a result influence and are influenced by others.

It is important for depressive people to understand that they cannot remain unchanged. *Change is not only possible; it is inevitable.* If you are depressed, your task is to make positive, hopeful changes that propel you toward a better tomorrow.

Each of us has a certain perspective on time that colors our experiences. This perspective is *learned.* Some folks focus on the past, perhaps because they have grown up valuing tradition. Others keep their eye on the future; they have been taught the value of setting goals and making plans. Still others spend most of their time responding to urgencies of the moment, putting out fires or satisfying their immediate needs. They are oriented to the present.

In my clinical experience, most depressed individuals are oriented to the past. They desperately need to envision and carve out a positive future. They also need to take steps toward that future.

This is not to ignore the past or fail to live in the present, but rather to embrace hope. By envisioning a positive future and acting to bring it about, one begins to conquer depression.

Psychologist Michael Yapko also believes that getting your time orientation out of whack can lead to depression. He writes that "it's all too typical of depressed thinking to see the future only as more of whatever is depressing you right now" (1990, 85).

Delving into the past has little value, **except to the degree that it reveals things you have done well (and can do again) and things you can learn to do better.**

Nothing can change the past. But you can learn new ways of responding to bad events. You can change your attitude or your assessment of a bad situation. Or you can simply begin to act differently.

Framing Hope

Life is an ambiguous situation from beginning to end. In the context of that ambiguity, we need to project meaning onto the events of our lives. Some people project that life is good. Some project pain to be endured on the screen of their lives. A few project no meaning at all: "Life's a bore, and then you die."

difficult task with sufficient energy to help guide the agency back to financial health. Hope came when I (reluctantly) reframed the problem into an opportunity.

In short: we can interpret events in our lives as neutral, good, or bad. Even serious problems can become opportunities for growth and greater strength if we frame them in a positive way. When you frame a situation positively (even if you don't observe it as accurately as an objective outsider might), you will feel better and gain more energy to do what needs to be done. It's the sensible thing to do.

Reframing Hope

Reframing turns liabilities into strengths. It constructs a new way to organize and view experiences—not through rose-colored lenses, but through the clear glass of reality.

Another word for *frame* might be *perspective*. Frames are the ways in which we perceive events or circumstances, and they shape our reality. The meaning of an event depends upon the frame of the person experiencing it. Different individuals may react to the same or similar situations with very dissimilar feelings, thoughts, behaviors, and attitudes.

To reframe an experience is to reinterpret it mentally and/or emotionally in a way that fits the facts of the situation as well or even better. Reframing can change the entire meaning of an event.

Harold feels bad that his daughter Tracy seldom calls him on the telephone. He thinks she doesn't love him, doesn't care how he is doing. I wasn't a very attentive father, Harold broods. Tracy must resent me for the way I neglected my family in years past.

What happens when he reframes this situation? Harold notices that his daughter works hard at her job and has many other responsibilities as well. He has time on his hands. Why doesn't he call her?

Harold gives it a try. Tracy sounds delighted to hear from him. At the end of their conversation she says, "Call me again—I loved talking with you! Call me collect!" Harold's new, realistic frame tells him that, while she is a little forgetful, it's not due to resentment or lack of love. There isn't a rule that says the child must be the one to initiate the call. Harold's opportunities for talking with Tracy are limited only by his telephone bill. Of course, he can always call her collect!

All right, I know what you're thinking. Tracy might just as well have been a selfish or resentful daughter. Not all real-life situations turn out as nicely as they do in books like this one, true enough. But this negative thought is itself an example of depressive thinking. You'd be surprised how often such situations *do* turn out nicely, once they are revisited with a positive interpretation. You'll never know until you try.

Reframing helps depressed people look for exceptions to the assumptions underneath their negative point of view. Once they entertain even the slightest doubt about any portion of the old frame—once they consider that there may be another way of looking at the event—they find it harder to return to their negative point of view. They begin to visualize a future that isn't dominated by the problem.

In a helpful example of positive reframing, religious writer Parker Palmer (1995, 327) described his battle with depression as a "school of the spirit." At the time, Palmer was seeing a spiritual director, a sort of personal guide to one's spiritual life, who suggested: "You can keep imaging depression as the hand of an enemy trying to crush you. But what about thinking of it instead as the hand of a friend trying to press you down to firm ground on which it's safe to stand?"

Palmer described how that new frame helped him to see his melancholy and his relationship with God differently. "God as ground has become a very powerful image for me. . . . If you feel yourself falling, it's probably because you started someplace other than God—someplace off the ground."

Please don't interpret this image as an angry God reaching down to correct an errant child with the blight of depression. But it may be helpful for some people to consider the possibility that God can use depression to serve some purpose—such as bringing one to firm ground. For the person of faith, God is present not only in the good times but also in times of suffering (see chapter 20). This is but one example of how to reframe a bad situation in a more positive way.

Depression: A Negative Frame on Experience

Daily, hourly, and minute-by-minute we are bombarded by an infinite number of images and data. This is in the nature of our biology, and it is multiplied by our high-tech, high-speed, information-driven society.

It is impossible to pay attention to every piece of data that assails your senses in the course of a day or even a minute. By necessity, we filter and select incoming messages in order to make our way through the jungle of information.

As we choose to frame events positively or negatively, therefore, we are never working with all of the information available to us. It is impossible to take it all in.

Do we have any choice over what we let in and what we screen out? Certainly we do. Recent research suggests that the filtering process is built-in, but that we can change our subconscious filter (Wilson 2002). Reframing can help depressed individuals recognize the positive elements in a situation—to see data they have been screening out because of their pessimistic world view—and thus to look at events from a more confident and realistic perspective.

Certain events, of course, are more difficult than others to frame in a positive way. They appear to offer little good. Michael faced such a challenge. He accepted a new job, sold the home he had inherited from his grandparents, moved his family across the country, and invested their life's savings in a new house. So Michael might have

A Little Advice as You Continue
to Work through This Book

The following chapters focus mainly on the four characteristics of depression—interpersonal, behavioral, physiological, and cognitive—discussed in chapter 3. As you continue reading, look for methods of change that match the characteristics of your depression. For example, if you have marital difficulties, interpersonal approaches (chapters 15 to 17) would be a good place to start.

Research studies on treating depression show that the best way to deal with depression is to target more than one of its characteristics. It is best to choose several methods of change—things you're sure you can do with success—in order to address more than one facet of your melancholia.

Change in any one of the symptom areas will naturally impact other areas. For example, thinking (chapters 9 to 11) and doing (chapters 12 to 14) often work hand-in-hand. And frequently a physiological change (chapters 6 through 8), like taking antidepressant medications, will benefit individuals no matter what their typical characteristics of depression are.

A tripod is more stable than a pogo stick. Triangulate your efforts—try three new skills, or even just two, plus medication if it's prescribed—to ensure broader and more lasting results. I suggest that you choose methods that seem most attractive, easily achievable, and appropriate for your unique symptoms and circumstances.

If you are depressed, you are probably stuck in the past, sense little freedom in the present, and see only a bleak future filled with more suffering. To be a vital human being not dominated by depression is to look beyond your immediate circumstances or past liabilities. It is to anticipate the future with the awareness that you have freedom—however limited—to become more of the person you can be, ought to be, deserve to be. It is to take responsibility for shaping that future.

Even in the depths of depression there is hope. Hope recognizes the past but also takes action in the present in order to move into a future that is all possibility. To act is to recapture hope, and thereby to revive faith in yourself, faith in life, and faith in the future.

TAKE ACTION

Take a virtual trip.

✓ Think of one small thing you would like to do differently. Take an evening class at a local community college, eat at a Thai restaurant, take your dog to obedience school, wear different clothes, or go on a weekend jaunt without the children.

✓ Whatever you would like to do differently, do it! Don't promise to do it forever; just try it on for size. If it doesn't fit, try something else.

FOR THE FAMILY

Take care of yourself and the family.

✓ Take the satisfaction in life quiz in the TAKE ACTION box at the end of the Introduction. If your score is very much lower than it usually would be, let it be a signal to tend your own needs.

✓ As much as possible, keep your family life in order. Continue with normal family activities.

✓ Be aware that you are more vulnerable to depression yourself at times like this. If you let yourself get towed under, you will be of no help to your loved one.

✓ If you are married and your marital relationship is less fulfilling than it once was, you may be tempted to experiment with relationships outside your marriage (physical or emotional). This is one more reason to live as normal a life as possible when a spouse is depressed.

✓ Don't withdraw from a depressed spouse or child—even if it feels as if the person is withdrawing from you.

✓ Keep up your satisfying hobbies, sports, and club or church activities; go to the movies, dine out, cook delicious meals—do whatever gives you satisfaction, hope, or meaning.

CHAPTER SIX

Body and Brain: The Physical Face of Depression

IN THIS CHAPTER YOU WILL:

✓ Find out what typically happens to your body during a depressive episode.
✓ Consider how body image affects mood.
✓ Learn to recognize depression "look-alikes."
✓ Note that changes in diet can also change mood.
✓ Refer to the list of foods that people suffering from melancholy best avoid, and those that may help alleviate depression.

Did you ever injure one part of your body and feel pain in another part? Did a single insect bite cause your entire arm to itch?

Not too long ago I bought a small, 1940s Craftsman metal lathe. It works on the same principle as a pottery wheel, spinning the piece you are working on while you shape it into a cylindrical form. (For a hobby I collect and restore antique radios, and I needed this tool for making metal parts that are no longer available.) As soon as I got the lathe working, I practiced turning a small piece of brass. My hand got too close to the spinning piece of metal. *Whack!* Besides the immediate pain in my hand, my whole arm hurt. I felt light-headed and wobbly-kneed.

> **My body (and yours) is a system. Whatever happens to one part of it, however small, affects the whole system. This includes what goes on in the brain: thoughts, feelings, attitudes, and urges.**

Fifty years ago, depression was generally considered to be a psychological or mental disorder. Now, most medical and mental health professionals agree that depression has a significant biological component. Physiology—the physical aspects of the body and brain—contributes to depression, even though we don't fully know the extent to which it does.

How do we know this? One clue is that depression runs in the family, at least some of the time. If one parent has a history of melancholia, the children are more likely than the general population to experience depression. When two parents have depression in their background, the children's chances are even greater. Researchers studying identical twins separated at birth have found that if one twin experiences depression the other is likely to become depressed as well, even though they have been raised in different family environments (DeBattista & Schatzberg 1995).

What Causes Depression?

Isabel gave birth to five children and bounced right back from the delivery—cooking, cleaning, mothering, and keeping up with her part-time job as a computer technician— less than thirty-six hours after each delivery. When she had her sixth baby, things didn't go so smoothly. For the first few weeks, she cried easily. She had no interest in taking care of little Emilio—or her other children, for that matter. Dishes piled up in the sink. Everyone pitched in to cook, straighten, and clean (sort of). But the nerve center of the household was down. Nothing operated smoothly. Isabel wondered if the family wouldn't be better off without her.

Everyone told her she was just a little older and would have to be patient with herself. Her husband and teenage children made her get dressed, took her out, and didn't take no for an answer when Isabel said she'd rather sleep. By Emilio's first birthday, she was pretty much her normal self, just a little toned-down.

Once Isabel had started to climb out of her valley and could think straight, she recalled something about her mother. Hilda was tired and despondent for two years following the birth of Isabel's younger sister. The family felt ashamed; they didn't talk about it in public, and Isabel's grandmother ran the household. Gradually Hilda got better, but she went through several similar slumps throughout the rest of her life. Was Isabel's depression inherited from her mother? Was there some relationship to childbirth?

The causes of depression are multiple and complex. They vary from person to person and situation to situation:

❑ Some people get depressed after only a few outside triggers, or none at all. They may report physical symptoms, such as sleep disturbance and fatigue, without feeling remarkably sad or down.

❑ Some people may endure a sea of troubles over a long period of time before depression overtakes them.

she needed to buy her sofa. Then, out of the blue, her husband brought home a brand new Harley Davidson motorcycle with a high-interest, five-year payment plan.

How would you react in Rita's situation? It would be normal to get angry, maybe yell and complain a little, or use the new Harley as an excuse to go ahead and buy the sofa on credit. For Rita, it prompted a free fall into despair.

In the following years, I saw Rita through several depressive episodes. Each one started with something that most eyes would see as a passing event—upsetting perhaps, but insignificant in the great scheme of things. Rita's body seemed wired for depression. Some chemical imbalance, perhaps, in the tissues of her brain made it difficult for her to respond normally to the passing stresses of her life.

Rita was one of those people who needs more than medication. She takes her antidepressants faithfully, but also has made significant changes in her life that have allowed her to live depression free for more than twenty years. On occasion, Rita still hears depression knocking at her door, but now she immediately gets active. She does the things that she has learned will mute the knocking and keep the blues outside in the cold.

Look out! There's a trap here. It can be comforting to know that there is a biological link to depression. Unfortunately, this knowledge can also become a way to rationalize irresponsible actions. I have seen depressed individuals who rest in the cradle of their genetic susceptibility to depression. They are helpless and passive. They refuse to make any changes in the way they live their lives. A good bumper sticker for such people would read: NOTHING CAN BE DONE, THEREFORE I WILL DO NOTHING.

It is vital for all of us—whether or not our depression is biologically based—to work at making changes in our actions, thinking, and relationships so that we will not be laid low by present or future episodes of depression. We also have a responsibility to do what we can to minimize depression's impact on our families, friends, and coworkers. A better bumper sticker would read: SOMETHING CAN BE DONE, THEREFORE I WILL DO SOMETHING.

My Image of My Body

Standing in the grocery checkout line, our eyes scan racks of magazines picturing lithe young women and trim, muscular men on the covers. It is the "ideal" image packaged and sold by the advertising, fashion, and entertainment industries. Standing before a full-length mirror, few of us can measure up. The ideal is not real. We need to value our bodies, to accept them realistically, and to resist comparing them to magazine covers.

Through the years, I have counseled a number of depressed people who view themselves as fat, unattractive, and unacceptable to others. Many tell me that they have been on dozens of diets. When they do lose weight, the pounds came back.

What helps people with a poor body image? First, I urge them *not* to go on a diet—just become more active. They should choose a physical activity that is fun, something they can do successfully. Anything that gets a person moving will qualify—bicycling, dancing, jogging, walking, swimming, racquet sports, one-on-one basketball sessions, aerobics classes, mall walking, working out at the gym, or gardening. Some people just resolve to climb stairs instead of riding the elevator and to park their car in the back of the lot.

One woman I know has a creative solution for days when she can't go out for a walk: she calls it "doing housework inefficiently." Instead of cleaning rooms one at a time, she does all of them at once, dashing from room to room and floor to floor. By the time the house is clean, she's had a workout!

Once the person has become more active, if they also want to do something about their weight, I usually suggest groups such as Overeaters Anonymous or Weight Watchers (depending on the nature of their overeating).

I do not recommend an immediate weight loss effort for the depressed because *more than ninety percent of people who lose weight gain it back again.* If you are depressed, the last thing you need is another failure. Weight loss is better undertaken in a more positive frame of mind, after you have faced your depression-related issues and put other changes in place.

Illness and Medication

We agree that depression isn't "all in your head." There's a chance it isn't in your head at all. A wide variety of ailments can cause fatigue and depression-like symptoms. These include the flu, cancer, asthma, chronic fatigue syndrome, severe allergies, migraine headaches, heart disease, malaria, infections, brain tumors, and much more.

Depression look-alikes

Some physical maladies are so exhausting that the patient feels unable to do much of anything, and therefore may be misdiagnosed as depression. Low thyroid can cause depression-like symptoms, as can Cushing's disease. Medical events (heart attack, heart surgery, stroke) may also bring on feelings or behaviors that look like depression.

Medicine that makes things worse

Some prescription drugs can cause depression or something depression-like as a side effect. These include some drugs for high blood pressure (such as Reserpine, Methyldopa, Hydralazine, and Propranolol) and anti-Parkinson's medications (such as Levodopa and Bromocriptine). If a medication triggers depression-like symptoms, your physician may be able to find another one that doesn't have this side effect. Or your doctor may decide that the depressive side effects of a particular drug outweigh its benefits, and take you off it entirely.

FOR THE FAMILY

Make dietary changes for the family.

If you do most of the cooking (or if you are the one who decides where you are going out to eat) you may be able to influence a diet change for the family. As an experiment for two or three weeks, try the dietary changes suggested in the TAKE ACTION box earlier in this chapter. To summarize:

✓ Eat a high-protein breakfast low in starch, sugar, and saturated fat.
✓ Eliminate caffeine.
✓ Eliminate alcoholic beverages, or restrict to one or two drinks per week.

Be flexible. Don't make the eating plan so restrictive that you're bound to abandon it. If you notice even slight changes for the better in your loved one's mood, continue with the new plan. You can get additional dietary information from a nutritionist, books such as *The South Beach Diet,* or on the Internet.

CHAPTER SEVEN

Physical Remedies

IN THIS CHAPTER YOU WILL:

✓ Focus on a fact that you probably already know: when depressed, people often have trouble sleeping and especially wake up early in the morning.

✓ Find some specific, concrete steps you can take to get a better night's sleep.

✓ Find out how to relax, if anxiety is part of your depression, using one or more of the relaxation methods suggested in these pages.

By now you know that depression has many physical symptoms. You've observed them in your own experience, or that of your loved one. There are also relatively simple, doable physical remedies that you can take to help overcome your low feelings. This chapter will suggest some of them.

Sleeping Better

After recovering from triple bypass heart surgery, Faye slowly regained her energy. She was glad to be alive. She had recovered enough to ask her doctor about returning to work when she was blindsided by an episode of depression. Women don't have heart attacks, she mistakenly thought; men do. It wasn't fair. First the heart attack, then surgery, and now depression.

Faye was pretty low when I met her. She had lived on adrenaline ever since she earned her MBA twenty years before, relishing the fast-forward life of bonds trading. She liked the pace, the travel to world capitals, the important people, the money. Now here she was in Arizona, living with her retired parents until she could recover and return to New York.

Life in Sun City had little resemblance to her other world. Of course Fay knew she had to make some changes in her life. She was already making them: walking every day, giving up cigarettes, drinking less alcohol, and eating healthier food. The improvement in her mood was noticeable, but she still experienced some sleep disturbance and a little embarrassing tearfulness (especially if she had not slept well the night before).

We decided to work on her sleep problems first. Loss of sleep afflicts a majority of depressed persons. But sleep disturbance is not just a symptom of depression; it also can be a cause.

Sleep deprivation makes you crazy. Mind-control experts use sleep disturbance to brainwash their victims. Prisoners of war who refuse to cooperate with their captors in spite of horrible physical torture often break down after being deprived of sleep.

Most people can handle a night or two without sleep, but after three nights they start feeling (and acting) crazy. They have memory loss and delusions. They are easily led and sometimes paranoid. Long-term sleep loss tends to cause confusion, fuzzy thinking, daytime sleeping, irritability, fits of anger, nervousness, and other problems that may intensify depression.

Let's say that you are depressed because of some physical malady. If you have abnormal sleep patterns and significant loss of sleep, your melancholia will almost certainly get worse. Prolonged sleep disturbance can transform a mild depression into a deep despondency.

Sleep disturbance takes several forms:

- ❏ You may wake early in the morning, perhaps at four o' clock, and stay awake until daylight. (This is one of the most common features of depression.)

- ❏ You may have difficulty falling asleep. You may have the kind of restless, shallow sleep from which you wake feeling as if you never really slept.

- ❏ You may sleep almost all the time (except, typically, at night).

If you are having difficulty sleeping, you need to do something about this first, before tackling your other issues.

Here's the good news about sleep disturbance: *You can do something about it.* Improving your night's sleep will give you more energy for managing and conquering your depression. Not only that, it is almost certain that, once you are sleeping better, you will already feel less depressed!

The following tips worked for Faye. They have helped a great many people back to normal sleep patterns. First take the suggestions that seem easiest to you, and do as many of them as you can do without failure or discomfort.

- ❏ *Use the bedroom only for sleep and sex*. This was easy for Faye. She took the TV out of the bedroom. Once in bed she does not work, study, or read (with the possible exception of some really boring reading material). If you sleep in a multipurpose room, apply this principle to the bed itself, if possible, creating a sleeping zone in one corner of the room.

- ❏ *If you are sleepy but wakeful, try to stay awake*. My wife uses this method. She lies perfectly still, opens her eyes, stares at a spot on the wall, and tries as hard and as long as possible to keep her eyes open. After a few seconds her eyelids get heavy, but she does her best to keep them open. Within minutes she's back asleep. When I passed the suggestion on to Faye, she laughed at me but promised to give it a try. It worked!

- ❏ *If you are not sleeping, get up*. Depressed people frequently lie awake in bed rehearsing their negative thoughts. Faye was amazed at how easy it is to simply get up and do something constructive. The occasional loss of a night's sleep is no worse than tossing and turning in bed, and it almost always helps you sleep better the next night.

- ❏ *Become more active during the day*. People who pass their time sitting, watching television, taking long naps, or surfing the Internet make it harder to sleep at night. It was easy for Faye to be active during her convalescence at her parents' home; it would be harder back in her New York office. Faye decided that after returning to work she would take frequent, short breaks to walk about the building. She would run errands for coworkers, taking the stairs instead of the elevator. Whenever possible, she would stand at her work station.

- ❏ *Do not take naps during the day*. Faye had to give up her 5:30 nap, but in return she feels sleepier at 11:00.

- ❏ *Take some regular, vigorous exercise*. Just don't do it within the last two hours before bedtime. The long-term effect of exercise is relaxing, but its immediate result is energizing and stimulating. In the past, Faye tended to have an evening slump, with a nap followed by little or no meaningful activity. Now her doctor-approved exercise session starts as soon as she walks in the door of her apartment. The exertion provides a boost of energy for her evening's tasks or recreation, and by bedtime it leaves her more relaxed. (More about exercise below.)

Keeping the other muscles of your body relaxed, extend your left arm straight out in front of you while pulling your hand back at the wrist. Hold it.

Sense the tension building. Wait.

Now relax your hand. Lower your arm while feeling the tension flowing out and the relaxation flowing in.

Let your arm and hand lie loose and limp, heavy and relaxed. Feel the relaxation.

Now become aware of both your arms and hands. Notice how they feel.

Keeping the other muscles of your body relaxed, extend both arms straight out in front of you.

Now make a tight fist with both hands. Hold it.

Sense the tension building. Wait.

Now relax your hands. Lower your arms while imagining and feeling the tension flowing out and the relaxation flowing in.

Let your arms and hands lie loose and limp, heavy and relaxed. Feel the relaxation.

Shift your attention to your right leg and foot.

Notice how they feel. Keeping the other muscles of your body relaxed, extend your right leg straight out in front of you and pull your right foot and toes back toward you. Hold it.

Sense the tension building. Wait.

Now relax your right foot and toes. Lower your leg while imagining and feeling the tension flowing out and the relaxation flowing in.

Let your right leg and foot be loose and limp, heavy and relaxed. Feel the relaxation.

Become aware of your left leg and foot. Notice how they feel. Keeping the other muscles of your body relaxed, extend your left leg straight out in front of you and pull your left foot and toes back toward you. Hold it.

Sense the tension building. Wait.

Now relax your left foot and toes. Lower your leg while imagining and feeling the tension flowing out and the relaxation flowing in.

Let your left leg and foot be loose and limp, heavy and relaxed. Feel the relaxation.

Now shift your attention to both your legs and feet. Notice how they feel. Keeping the other muscles of your body relaxed, extend both legs straight out in front of you while pressing your feet and toes forward. Hold it.

Sense the tension building. Wait.

Now relax your feet and toes. Lower your feet and legs while imagining and feeling the tension flowing out and the relaxation flowing in.

Let your legs and feet be loose and limp, heavy and relaxed. Feel the relaxation.

Now become aware of your chest and abdomen. Notice how they feel. Keeping the other muscles of your body relaxed, tightly pull in your abdomen and expand your chest. Hold it.

Sense the tension building. Wait.

Now relax your abdomen and chest while imagining and feeling the tension flowing out and the relaxation flowing in.

Let your chest and abdomen be loose and limp, heavy and relaxed. Feel the relaxation.

Now shift your attention to your back. Notice how it feels. Keeping the other muscles of your body relaxed and your breathing calm and regular, pull your shoulders straight back while gently arching your upper back backward, allowing your abdomen and pelvis to go forward. Hold it.

Feel the tension building. Wait.

Now relax your back while imagining and feeling the tension flowing out and the relaxation flowing in.

Let your entire back be loose and limp, heavy and relaxed. Feel the relaxation.

Now shift your attention to your shoulders, neck, and face. Notice how they feel. Keeping the other muscles of your body relaxed, raise your shoulders up toward your ears, keeping your lower arms relaxed, and gently press your head backward while clenching your jaws tightly together and squeezing your eyelids closed. Hold it, but keep breathing.

Feel the tension building. Wait.

Now lower your shoulders, relax your neck, jaws, eyes, and your entire face while imagining and feeling the tension flowing out and the relaxation flowing in.

Let your shoulders and neck be loose and limp, heavy and relaxed, your jaw loose and slack, your eyes relaxed and calm, and your entire face soft and relaxed. Feel the relaxation in your shoulders, neck, and face.

Now scan over your entire body and sense the good feelings of relaxation that exist in your mind and body.

Now I'm going to count, slowly, from one to five. At the count of five, take a deep breath. When inhaling, mentally say, "Mind alert, wide awake," and open your eyes. On the exhale say, "Relaxed and refreshed."

One. Coming up. Two. Three. Four. Five.

Breathe in deeply. Say, "Mind alert, wide awake," and open your eyes.

Exhale, saying, "Relaxed and refreshed."

Gently stretch all your muscles, then slowly get up, feeling alert and refreshed.

During the period of five to seven seconds when the muscles are held tense, they should be quite tight but never to the point of pain. At the beginning, you do not have to cover all of the parts of your body; as you practice and sharpen you ability to relax, you will be able to do more.

The effective use of progressive relaxation requires that you consider your special needs or physical conditions. When you become familiar with the method, you can reduce the amount of detail in the description of how to relax particular muscle groups. Eventually you may not need the tape to do your relaxation routine.

Practice once or twice a day for about fifteen minutes until you learn to relax quickly. It's best to do one session soon after you awake in the morning, and one in the evening.

You are learning a skill much like learning to drive a car; there is nothing magical to it. By taking a let-it-happen attitude, you allow yourself to relax without forcing it. You won't upset yourself if it doesn't happen right away.

Other Relaxation Methods

The slow, step-by-step process described above is necessary in the early stages of learning to relax. Once you learn the basic steps, you can use additional methods that will apply the learning more widely in your daily life and shorten the time it takes to relax.

Full body progressive relaxation

This advanced exercise requires only one or two minutes. It is especially helpful for those who are able to relax with the progressive relaxation method. It involves simultaneously tensing as many muscles in your body as you are capable of tensing.

Stand on your tiptoes, clench your fists, scrunch up your face, raise your shoulders, and tip your head back. Tighten as many other muscle groups as possible for five to seven seconds. Then let all muscles go limp for fifteen seconds and sense the feeling of relaxation. This method works best when used two or three times in succession.

Breathing exercise

Close your eyes and monitor your breathing, focusing on the exhale. Mentally say at each inhale "I am," and at each exhale, "letting go." Do this for a few minutes and notice how your breathing slows down and you feel more calm and relaxed.

Or try a variation of this method: sit calmly, close your eyes, and focus on exhaling through the nose. On each exhale repeat the words "calm" or "relax." As you continue to do this, the pairing of relaxation with the words "calm" or "relax" is reinforced. In the future, the mental repetition of these words at tense moments in a busy day can bring instant relaxation.

Mini-vacation

Do one of the exercises above and then visualize a relaxing place or event, one that is intended to calm rather than excite. For example, you may see yourself floating on an inflatable raft on a quiet, sunny lake, feeling the warmth of the sun on your skin, the smell of the lake, the sound of the wind blowing through the pine trees on shore. Make sure you choose a scene that would be relaxing for *you*, not someone else. Let your imagination go and allow all of your senses to become alive. This exercise provides a mini-vacation in the midst of a stressful day.

Meditation and spiritual direction

Any form of relaxation practice can be coupled with meditative time or one of the classic spiritual disciplines, such as prayer or reflection on a passage of scripture. The two complement and enhance each other. (If you want to read more, look at a book like *Full Catastrophe Living* by Jon Kabot-Zinn.)

Exercise: *Just Do It!*

I hate jogging. Swimming is boring. Stationary bicycles aren't much better, but at least you can watch CNN. The hard part is convincing yourself to do it regularly. Therefore it is important to find an activity that offers fun as well as cardiovascular benefits. For example, you might get a dog and take it for daily walks. The dog will certainly appreciate it. In all likelihood your pooch will beg for its daily walk, making it more difficult for you to skip a day and then another and another.

You don't have to pound the pavement or swim laps. Any regular cardiovascular exercise helps keep depression at bay. My personal choice was racquet sports until two blown knees sidelined me to weight machines and easy walking trails.

- ❏ Go rollerblading.

- ❏ Garden.

- ❏ Take up a dog/human sport like canine agility.

- ❏ Breakdance. Tango. Dance in the pool.

- ❏ March naked around the living room to the tune of your favorite music (pull the drapes first).

- ❏ Throw horseshoes till your arm drops off.

- ❏ Mow the lawn.

- ❏ Two-step across Texas.

> **No matter what you do, *just do it!* Activity is your good buddy.
> It helps you control your sad and dark moods.**

Why is exercise so good for us? Physically fit people are stronger and more energetic, for one thing. Regular exercise offers a sense of accomplishment: "here is something I can do; it introduces some discipline into my life." Discipline gives a sense of self-control to melancholics who feel they have no power over anything in their lives.

Anything active—even housecleaning or picking up trash along your designated two miles of highway—can serve as a distraction from obsessive negative thinking and shift your focus to positive thoughts.

If you haven't been in the habit of exercising, start very small. A good rule of thumb for pacing yourself: you should feel the effort but still be able to carry on a conversation (real or hypothetical) while you are exercising. If you have pain, stop. If the pain continues, take an extra day off and use the RICE cure (rest, ice, compression, and elevation). If the pain continues, see a physician.

Exercising every day will be most effective against anxiety. But if you're not going to do it daily, write a plan for yourself that includes days off so you won't ever feel that you've blown it.

Above all, whether you're working on your sleep problems, relaxation training, exercise, or any other self-improvement program, go easy on yourself. *What you need most is success!*

Try not to take on too many changes at first. Do what you can do without piling on additional stress. You know you ought to give up smoking or lose weight, but it may be too much to think about while you are taking steps toward managing depression. Be wary about making difficult or sweeping changes.

Treat yourself kindly, like an old and valued friend. Give yourself some slack, but *never give up*. Decide to do whatever you are sure you can do. Then do it.

TAKE ACTION

Sleep disturbance, tension, and lack of exercise often make depression worse.

✓ If you are waking up early most mornings, follow the suggestions on pages 77–78. Observe (and jot in your notebook) instances of sleeping better and feeling better after just a few days of doing them.

✓ Begin practicing a relaxation exercises. Choose one that makes sense to you—either one of those discussed in this chapter or one that was helpful to you in the past .

✓ If you find you have even the slightest improvement in your sleeping, continue doing these exercises.

✓ If you see no improvement after trying one of these suggestions for a month, you can give it up and try something else.

FOR THE FAMILY

Regular exercise has been shown to improve mood.

✓ Exercise with your family member who is struggling with depression. It will provide benefits for both of you.

✓ Try to find an activity that offers fun for both of you (along with providing cardiovascular benefits). Any regular heart/lung exercise will help keep depression and caregiver burnout at bay.

✓ Tell yourself you will exercise for a month, not for the rest of your lives.

✓ If your loved one doesn't want to go with you to walk the dog, go yourself—then ask again the next time.

✓ Don't give up after the first or second or even third turndown. Once a foot crosses the threshold, inertia is broken. Once your loved one takes even one brisk walk, you may see an elevation in mood. Once exercise becomes a habit, it gets easier.

Chemicals called neurotransmitters (literal translation: "nerve cell transport") are the boats that carry stuff from one island (neuron) to another. Where do they unload? At the dock! These docks are called receptors—specific places on each neuron where the neurotransmitters can deliver the information from the home neuron.

Just as there are many types of boats, the brain has several types of neurotransmitters. Monoamine neurotransmitters are the boats that ferry messages about thinking and feeling across the synapses. Three common monoamine neurotransmitters linked to your mood are serotonin, norepinephrine, and dopamine. A person is susceptible to depression when any of these monoamine neurotransmitters are faulty or insufficient, or when there is a problem with the receptors (docks) in the neurons.

Antidepressant medications are designed to correct problems with your brain's boats and docks. They increase the availability of neurotransmitters (boats) so that the neurons operate the way they should. After they have relayed the message from one neuron to the other, neurotransmitters break down and return to the originating neuron (home port). All of this, of course, happens at mind-boggling speed.

Some antidepressant drugs slow down the process, on the assumption that at higher speeds there may not be enough monoamine neurotransmitters to do the job. In other words, one barge might do the job of six speedboats. That barge can be pretty useful if you only have two or three speedboats available!

Sometimes a boat gets lost or malfunctions; it makes a U-turn before reaching the dock and goes back home without delivering its cargo. This tendency to return to home port is called re-uptake. The solution is to close down the homeport. Re-uptake inhibitors, some of the most common, recently-developed medications, keep the boat from returning home. It has nowhere to go but to its destination, where it can deliver its cargo.

Of course, these medications do not work exactly the same way for all people. There are a few stories out there about people's bad experiences with antidepressants—even concerns that taking the medications may lead to suicide. But more often than not the stories are miracle stories.

If you suffer from depression, only your physician can choose an antidepressant for you. I will not tell you to take these medications, and I certainly will not tell you what type you ought to take. But if you understand some of the more common ones, and how they work, you will be able to make informed decisions about them.

The beauty of antidepressants is that they treat the physiological (physical, biological) aspects of depression. They are designed to fix what's not working properly in the brain. As a result, they can be used together with the practical steps described in this book that address the other three arenas of depression (thoughts, behaviors, and relationships).

Like Cynthia, many people struggling with depressed feelings think that antidepressant medications act quickly, like aspirin or Valium. In fact, they function in an entirely different way. Aspirin reaches its peak efficiency in about thirty minutes and wears off in about four hours. It takes *ten days to four weeks* of taking an adequate dose for antidepressant medications to achieve their intended effect, and some doctors think it may be two months before the drug makes its full impact.

When you stop taking these pills, it takes weeks for their residual effects to disappear. So if Norman says, "I stopped taking my pills and I feel better," he may be correct—temporarily. The side effects of the medication are reduced, and the residual effects of the drug are still at work. But in time the lingering effects of the medication will wear off. If Norman has made no other changes in his life, his depression almost certainly will return. Then, if he decides to resume taking antidepressants, there will be another long period of buildup before its peak effectiveness returns. If he experienced side effects when he first started taking the drug, Norman most likely will experience them again. He's likely to regret that he stopped.

Types of Antidepressants

To visualize the way different kinds of antidepressants work, let's return to the image of a blue Canadian lake. A really big one, such as Lake of the Woods in Ontario and Minnesota, may have thousands of islands. Many of the islands within an hour's boat ride from a town are inhabited. This means houses built and repaired, wells dug, septic systems installed. A mail carrier makes the rounds of the islands. People boat to town for shopping and entertainment, visit friends and relatives on nearby islands.

One kind of boat will not serve all these purposes. At the very least, you'll need a barge for building materials, a powerful motorboat for getting to town quickly or delivering the mail, and perhaps a canoe for paddling over to the next island. People may also keep pontoon boats, sailboats, kayaks, and even paddleboats at their shores.

Likewise, physicians can choose between several types of medications to alleviate depression. This is important because several different malfunctions can occur in the neurons and neurotransmitters, requiring different kinds of "boats" to correct the problem.

Although several new-generation medications fall outside the following categories, this discussion will focus on the three major types of antidepressants that are popularly known as MAOIs, TCAs, and SSRIs.

Monoamine oxidase inhibitors (MAOIs)

Metabolism is the process of energy production, breakdown, and waste. Monoamine oxidase works to slow the metabolizing of the neurotransmitters dopamine, norepinephrine, and serotonin. By slowing down the metabolizing of these three "boats," thus delaying their breakdown and waste, MOAIs increase their presence in the synapses of the brain.

The MAOIs, first introduced in 1956, include phenelzine (Nardil), tranylcypromine (Parnate), and selegiline (Deprenyl), among others. MAOIs are effective antidepressants,

Among the SSRIs and other recent drugs that target serotonin and some other neurotransmitters are Paxil, Luvox, Serzone, Effexor, Remeron, Wellbutrin, and Reboxetine, to name a few.

Lithium carbonate

Finally, there is an old-time favorite: lithium carbonate. Lithium, not one of the three major types of medications discussed above, has had almost miraculous results with bipolar disorders (characterized by wide mood swings from elation and hyperactivity to deep despondency). Some studies, with research still underway, suggest that lithium is effective against major depression, and it is reported to help individuals with bipolar disorder in the depressed phase. In some cases, lithium at low dosages, combined with tricyclic medications, is reported to help more than 50 percent of individuals who at first do not respond to TCAs or MAOIs alone (Potter, Rudorfer, & Manji 1991).

This has been a very general overview of some of the more common pharmaceutical agents used to treat depression at the time this book went to press. The purpose has not been to list all of the possible actions, side effects, doses, or drug interactions. After all, several new antidepressants are released every year. Furthermore, I am not a physician.

It's your right to know!	**You should always request that your doctor review all of this information with you when prescribing antidepressant medication, and at regular intervals thereafter. Do not hesitate to ask for this information in writing from your doctor if he or she does not offer it routinely.**

Other treatments may be recommended in addition to or instead of the antidepressants mentioned above, depending on the most distressing symptoms of your particular depressive picture and the training and experience of your physician. These additional medications might include thyroid supplements, psychostimulants such as Ritalin, antipsychotic medications for psychotic, delusional, or agitated depressions, and mood stabilizers.

Taking Your Pills

If you are depressed, it is not your task (or your family's task) to determine whether you need to take medication. However, the following considerations may help you work with your primary care physician or psychiatrist in assessing the need for antidepressants. These factors may be especially useful for readers who want to direct a depressed loved one to the best possible care.

The greatest drawback of antidepressants is the tendency of depressed people to take their pills erratically, or stop taking them altogether. This increases the possibility of unpleasant side effects and minimizes or wipes out the benefits.

No single antidepressant is clearly superior to the others. There is not a pill on the market that will benefit all people. If one medication does not work, there is likely to be another one that does. Talk with your doctor about prescribing a different antidepressant in case the first one has intolerable side effects or fails to provide relief after a suitable period of time.

Doctors advise that a person who wants to get the full benefit of an antidepressant medication take it daily as prescribed, and keep on taking it for up to twelve months after the depressive symptoms have receded. Therefore it is important to consult with your prescribing physician before abruptly stopping antidepressant medication for any reason. Call your physician immediately to discuss your concern. Very often a simple dosage change or management strategy (such as taking the largest dose of the day right before going to bed if the pills make you sleepy, or adding more water and fiber or a mild stool softener to your regimen if you become constipated) can manage the side effects effectively.

At some point, your doctor may recommend that you taper off of the drug. This will depend on your medical history, the nature of your depression, and what medication you are taking. If your depressive episode was severe or recurrent, or if there is a family history of depression, your doctor may recommend that you continue at a lower maintenance dose for a longer period of time.

> **Be aware that some health maintenance organizations (HMOs) have limited the use of new-generation antidepressants in order to control spiraling drug costs. If you experience significant side effects from one of the older medications, your doctor may be able to advocate with your HMO for the use of a newer, more expensive medication in your particular case, even if it's not on the insurance company's formulary of approved drugs.**

There is no way to ensure that all physicians clearly explain these important guidelines to their depressed patients—or that the patients hear them. That's why it is a good idea to *bring a family member or close friend along* when you visit a doctor for your depression. Two sets of ears is better than one; that person may ask important questions that didn't occur to you.

It is also important to choose a doctor who can communicate effectively. Less than half of primary care physicians treating depressed people spent three or more minutes discussing it with them, a 1993 Rand Corporation study determined (Cowley 1994, 42). This

Overgeneralization

As the term indicates, depressives can draw sweeping conclusions about themselves, their worth, and their abilities from a few isolated incidents. A big-league pitcher struggling with depression goes through a slump (it happens to every athlete at one time or another); he then overgeneralizes and concludes that his career is over, the fans hate him, he's a bad father, and a no-good bum.

Exaggeration and minimization

In the midst of depression, people have difficulty perceiving events accurately. They tend to enlarge small, negative events way out of proportion. At the same time, they minimize their positive accomplishments.

During a performance review, Nan's supervisor mentions in passing that the company prefers its employees to dress more formally than Nan is accustomed to doing. Because she is struggling with depression, Nan exaggerates his offhand remark and thinks she is failing at her job and soon to be fired because of her "shoddy" appearance. At the same time, she minimizes her accomplishments and can't even hear the many positive comments her supervisor has made.

Personalization

The depressed may take responsibility for unfavorable events when there is little or no basis for such a connection. Juan and his family lose their house and everything they own in a Gulf coast hurricane. He descends into melancholia and blames himself for their losses because he did not accept a job offer in San Antonio years before. Clearly, Juan is personalizing the disaster. He is taking responsibility for events utterly beyond his control.

Either/or thinking

In the grips of depression, people have a tendency to think in absolutes. They categorize all that they do in one of two opposite positions: perfect or defective, all or nothing, immaculate or filthy, and so forth. Their world is like my border collie: all black and white.

Of course, nobody can ever attain absolute goodness or perfection, so it's almost automatic for the depressed to see themselves as bad or defective. In attempting to be perfect they fail miserably and spiral into deeper depression, lacking a realistic sense of the gray areas in which we live most of our lives. Depressed individuals who engage in either/or thinking assume that, if they are unacceptable by their own estimation, others—and that includes God—cannot accept them either.

Very few depressed people are pessimistic about everything. Most of them tend to be sensitive to certain triggers that set their negative thinking in motion.

Sometimes childhood incidents serve as the basis for negative beliefs about oneself, the future, and the external world. These negative concepts may be buried, but they come to life as a result of some specific new event that resembles those bad childhood experiences.

However, even though past experiences can lead a person to misinterpret events, *it is not necessary to explore the past in order to bring about change.* In fact, as we will discuss below, those who suffer from depression spend altogether too much time thinking about the past and not enough time actively functioning in the present or planning and working for the future.

Information Processing Errors

Peter was a pastor who struggled with melancholia. His worldview was already dark when 9/11 and the prospect of war in Afghanistan plunged him into the abyss. Peter announced to his family in early December that it would be wrong to have a festive Christmas while so much of the world was suffering. There would be no tree, no carols, no gifts. They would mark Christmas with prayer, self-examination, and fasting. His wife and children were devoted Christians who also felt disturbed by world events. They admired Peter's resolve, and complied willingly (but sadly, with a real sense of loss) to his dismal Christmas observance.

Sometimes the cognitive distortions of the depressed are so subtle that others—even family members—fall for them. Peter's wife and children didn't understand that he was denying his family a festive Christmas not only out of a keen social conscience, but out of his distorted, melancholic thinking.

People in the low places of depression mentally skew what is happening around them and firmly believe in the accuracy of their twisted perceptions. Whether you struggle with depression or have a family member who does, you need to be aware of some of the common ways in which depression causes people to misinterpret experience.

Concrete thinking

Often the depressed look for specific, concrete objects of blame for their distress. Garrett's romance breaks up, and he exclaims, "Women! You can't trust 'em!" His buddies chime in sympathetically. Garrett does not see the multitude of factors that contribute to a failed relationship, such as work pressures, circumstances, family, his own behavior and, yes, one particular woman.

Sierra tells her husband, "Bosses are all alike. My supervisor is making my life miserable—he's out to get me, just like the others." Out of loyalty and ignorance, her husband buys it. (It turns out that Sierra had problems under her previous supervisors as well, and might want to examine the way she responds to people in authority.)

The remedy for such concrete thinking is to understand the context, and then to recognize (for example) that different people in authority act in different ways, that not all women treat their lovers badly.

Assessment

First you need to discover the core negative assumptions or erroneous beliefs that you hold about yourself, others, and the world. Alexis, for example, thought she was incompetent, her customers inconsiderate (and possibly criminal), and the world around her filled with danger. She needed to root out every case of emotional reasoning, either/or thinking, and other information processing errors that she could find.

Learning

Exposing cognitive misconceptions tends to be the easier part of the process; the next task is to begin changing them. Alexis eventually learned to recognize her negative thinking patterns, but it took more persistence and determination to restate them realistically. Even with help from her counselor and the self-help book she was reading, Alexis had to work hard at relearning her automatic, pessimistic thoughts. It took effort to think neutrally or positively: "I don't have enough information to know why that man is scowling. Maybe he worked all night or had a fight with his wife or just hasn't had his coffee yet. If he was going to rob me, he wouldn't be paying with his credit card."

Practicing

The third step of cognitive restructuring moves from learning about negative misconceptions to catching them as they occur. Alexis needed to recognize her own information processing errors and then rethink them based on real, hard evidence. At times she had to tell herself that she didn't have enough information to jump to a conclusion; the funny sound in her engine, for example, could mean trouble or it could just be that she needed a tune-up.

Sometimes practicing means actively finding accurate information and then replacing the distorted thinking with thoughts that are more congruent with reality. Before thinking the worst, the next time Alexis heard a strange sound under the hood of her car, she would bring it to her brother-in-law for a diagnosis, or at least an educated opinion.

You may not be able to catch your cognitive misconceptions right away—sometimes not for several days. If you find yourself suddenly swamped with a wave of depression, stop and mentally move backward to discover the trigger of the depression (if there is one). Try to identify your automatic unrealistic thoughts and beliefs. Remember that it is important not only to discover information processing errors, but also to *replace them with realistic thinking*. The goal is to believe the new reality-based thoughts. If you can't manage that at first, at least *act as if* you believe them. It is surprising how quickly you will begin to believe these new reality-based thoughts.

Andrea was depressed when she visited me several years ago. She thought she had failed miserably in raising her daughter, Crystal. She should have spent more time with Crystal, given her piano lessons, encouraged her to participate in extracurricular activities, helped her fill out her college applications. Andrea gave herself quite an emotional flogging. Her negative inner critic had the upper hand, and she was miserably depressed.

When the torrent of self-accusation eased up for a moment, I asked: "What has brought you here now?" After another round of self-attack she revealed that Crystal had been accepted to several good colleges but Cornell, the school of her choice, had turned her down "and it's all my fault."

Andrea distorted her thinking in several ways. With *selective focus* she targeted one small detail and ignored all she had done for her daughter. (Crystal had recovered from her disappointment by the time Andrea came to see me and was happily planning her graduation party.) Andrea *overgeneralized*, drawing conclusions about her self worth from one incident. She *exaggerated* one relatively unimportant incident out of proportion. She also *personalized* the event, taking responsibility for her daughter's rejection by Cornell.

Once Andrea discovered the ways in which she had distorted her thinking about the situation, she constructed more reality-based thoughts. She tried hard to catch herself at taking blame for everything that went wrong in Crystal's life. She begged to disagree with her old way of thinking. She took into account the realistic limitations of her control. As a result, Andrea's depression and hand wringing diminished. She gained energy to do the things she wanted to do.

Sometimes you can practice realistic thinking by taking yourself through a sort of guided daydream. Imagine a difficult situation in your mind before actually facing it in real life. This in turn will help you recognize the negative distortions in your thinking. For example: picture yourself going through all of the steps involved in a certain activity and then try to predict specific roadblocks and potential conflicts that might arise while actually doing the activity. As you move through the image, catch yourself making cognitive misconceptions and attempt to correct them on the spot. Pay attention to every detail. Then work out strategies for doing the same thing in real life.

Finally, be kind to yourself; you may not perform up to your standards the first time.

Changing to more reality-based thinking is not only necessary for combating depression, but it *feels* better to have a more positive view of yourself, events, and the world. If you make the mistake of seeing things too positively on occasion, I promise you that you will *feel better* than if you continue to see things negatively. Maybe the glass is half empty, but you will *feel better* if you think it is half full.

Negative thinking patterns are one of the most common features of depression. Luckily, they are among the most readily corrected. As soon as you recognize areas where your thinking is clouded by pessimism, you can learn how to rethink the events in positive or at least neutral terms. But the real release will come *when you actually practice it.* You will catch your habitual negativity in midair. Maybe only once the first day, then two or three times, then every hour, and so on until the pessimism no longer dominates the way you interpret your world. Unchained from negativity, your present is freedom and your future is possibility.

TAKE ACTION

Discover your erroneous thinking patterns.
✓ Learn the common information processing errors (see above).
✓ Practice catching errors in your thinking process. Go on a hunting expedition; seek them out. Write them in your journal or notebook.
✓ Every time you catch yourself in an information processing error, replace it with realistic, reality-based thinking. Describe your new thinking in your journal.

The following worksheet may help you catch those pesky information processing errors and replace them with more realistic, reality-based thinking. Write down this form in your notebook that you carry around with you, or make a form on your computer.

Original Thought:

Information Processing Error:

Reality-Based Thought:

Revised Action:

For more help in rooting out distortions in your thinking and learning how to reverse them, see Paul Hauck's *Overcoming Depression* (1976), Albert Ellis and Robert Harper's *A New Guide to Rational Living* (1977), or my *Brief Pastoral Counseling* (1994).

FOR THE FAMILY

Family members need to catch erroneous thinking too.

As you read this chapter, did some of the information processing errors ring a bell with you? If so, it may be an interesting experiment to try and root out your own information processing errors and replace them with more realistic, information-based thinking. Try the exercise listed above in the TAKE ACTION box. Doing so will enable you to help yourself and your depressed family member begin thinking more clearly and realistically.

CHAPTER TEN

Those Negative Thoughts Keep Running through My Head

IN THIS CHAPTER YOU WILL:

✓ Examine those obsessive negative thoughts that often bedevil the depressed.
✓ Recognize that these negative thoughts are controllable through a series of methods that can squelch them, such as write, read, and burn; thought stopping; and yellow tablet analysis.
✓ Learn ways to create positive thinking once you know how to defeat obsessive pessimistic thinking.

Even if you're not depressed, you may have had some experiences with groundless, unpleasant thoughts. Here's a little true story about one of these times.

"Hamburger Face"

I was out bass fishing. My wife, Karen, sat home in bed, ice packs on her chest, recovering from a recent auto accident that could have been much, much worse. Christine, nine at the time, was outside riding her new bike with friends in our safe suburban neighborhood.

The doorbell rang. A neighbor stood on the porch, looking stricken. "Your daughter has been in a bike accident; we think she was hit by a car!" Karen's pain vanished as she ran down the street. There lay Christine next to her smashed bike, blood and tears streaming down her face. Neighbors had heard the screech of tires; if there was a car, it was long gone. Everyone's best guess was that she had a near miss, or perhaps a glancing blow, and went over the handlebars while the driver sped away.

A family friend agreed to drive them to the emergency room. While they waited for him to arrive, Karen tried to hold Christine firmly so she would calm down. Three times this slip of a girl broke her mother's iron grip, sprinted to the bathroom mirror, stared at her reflection, and screamed, "My face looks like hamburger!" Each time, Karen had to drag her back to the living room and try to calm her down again.

The nurses cleaned Christine's face, and the doctor pronounced her well enough to go home with only a mild concussion and the need for some dental work. Still she kept going to the mirror. Every time she saw her temporarily ruined face, she would cry out that it looked like hamburger. The sight upset her terribly, but she couldn't resist looking.

It wasn't until later in the day, when Christine was too exhausted to be anything but quiet, that Karen could convince her of the need to stay away from mirrors for a few days. By the next week, her face had healed enough that she could look in a mirror without calling herself "hamburger face."

Why do we have to focus on our misery?

What is the fascination with our injury and pain?

Why must we run to the mirror, when it makes us feel so bad?

One of the pitfalls of the depressed is the tendency to wallow in their problems. They focus on what's wrong in their past—fear, anxiety, abuse, victimization, inertia, sorrow, people they've hurt, people who've hurt them, missed opportunities, failure, unfair treatment, inadequacy, bad decisions, messed-up lives.

Some people recite their list of ills to a counselor, session after session, hoping to find insight and therefore relief. Unfortunately, such recitations seldom help—and when they do help, they take many, many sessions. It's not unheard of for depressed persons to spend literally hundreds of fifty-minute sessions rehashing their painful and disappointing past with a psychotherapist.

Perhaps your own experience has shown you what many psychotherapists (and research studies) report: that focusing on the negatives from your past not only doesn't help—it actually makes depression worse. It drags you down.

The past is of little use if you are struggling to gain relief from depression, except to capture from it some instances of strength, success, and hope, however small. How did you feel when you handled a problem well? What did you do then that is different from what you're doing now? What were the circumstances? How could you do it again today? How can you use those past skills in your present situation?

With that exception, the only hope for overcoming depression is to focus on the future, to envision a future that is not dominated by depression, to construct a future that is not perfect, to be sure, but satisfying and possible.

❑ First, it objectifies your concerns. It makes them more clear-cut and manageable.

❑ Second, it converts the obsessive thought from a forbidden taboo to a required chore, one of your daily tasks. I suppose it's only human to shun chores and gravitate towards the forbidden.

❑ Third, you are less likely to dwell on obsessive thoughts throughout the day when you've scheduled a time for them. Eventually more important matters will rise to the surface of your mind, and the negative, obsessive ruminations will sink lower and lower until they are far in the background.

"Write, Read, and Burn" is useful for controlling obsessive negative thoughts of all sorts—not only those concerning divorce. It works for bad memories of actual events as well as imagined slights, fears, resentments, thoughts about your worthlessness or inadequacy, or any other ruminations that drag you down.

Thought stopping

It is impossible to actively think about two different things at the same time. Think of it: when you were excited about summer vacation, you had difficulty concentrating in school. Your mind kept moving into the future, thinking about three months of freedom.

Thought stopping is based on this principle. It is an effective mode of relief for people who find it hard to dispel their negative, obsessive thoughts.

Did you forget to sign your tax return? What are you going to do about an upcoming bill that you can't afford to pay? Why has your child's teacher asked you to come in for a conference? Your obsessive thoughts don't have to be about earth-shaking subjects to keep you miserable in the daytime and awake at night.

❑ Sit back, close your eyes, and breathe. Take a few minutes to relax (perhaps using one of the relaxation exercises in chapter 7).

❑ Now visualize a mundane image that poses no threat—for example, sitting in your living room and reading the newspaper.

❑ Keep on thinking about it until the image is fully developed. Then shout out loud, "Stop!" Don't murmur—*yell*. (You may want to warn your housemates in advance.) Do this three or four more times.

❑ Once you feel comfortable with the first step, bring to mind one of your most common but least troubling negative thoughts. When you have it clearly in mind, yell, "Stop!"

❑ Keep practicing. Notice that, for one moment at least, the obsessive thought is banished by the shout. Why? Because *your brain can't think both things at once*. It really can't. It's impossible.

❑ After you have yelled "Stop!" five or six times, again bring to mind the same obsessive thought, but this time don't say "Stop!" out loud. Shout it silently, in your mind. In the next few repetitions, *alternate* between shouting "Stop!" and thinking it.

❑ When you are able (momentarily) to dispel the troublesome thought at will, only shout "stop" in your head, without saying a word out loud.

❑ Practice this until it works consistently.

❑ Next, include thoughts that are even more troubling and practice stopping them until finally you are able to stop your most worrisome and obsessive thoughts at will.

You can see how changing to an unspoken cue makes the exercise more useful. You can't be yelling "Stop!" at the top of your lungs in the supermarket. Your coworkers might take a dim view of it in the office. But you can shout it silently in the subway or the classroom, at a dinner party, or even in a house of worship.

Here are two suggestions to enhance your success in thought stopping. First, practice it for five minutes three times a day, purposely bringing obsessive thoughts to mind and then banishing them with the thought-stopping procedure. Second, once you have it down, use silent thought stopping every time you find yourself obsessing about something. If negative thoughts pop up . . . "Stop!"

Problems? You may have difficulty setting aside time to practice thought stopping. You may find it hard to believe it will work. Thought stopping seems a little like hocus-pocus, and most people do not believe in magic.

Keep in mind, however, that there are good physiological reasons why thought stopping works. Your brain cells cannot actively think two thoughts at the same moment. (Sorry, all you multi-taskers.) Don't abandon the method because you feel silly doing it. Maybe that's why it works! Practice it. You'll appreciate the results.

Yellow tablet analysis

Years ago, one of my professors warned his students not to "analyze until you paralyze." He was really talking to certain individuals in the class who would turn over every rock—every word, phrase, thought, and inference, no matter how small—to look for hidden meanings and fault.

Woody Allen created one of these characters, Mickey Sachs, in the movie *Hannah and Her Sisters*. Analyzing every ache and twinge in his body had turned him into a hypochondriac obsessed with the fear that he had one malignancy or another.

The same tendency toward incessant, obsessive analysis can make people prone to depression. They may spend hours, days, weeks, even years looking under rocks. They examine every aspect of their lives—rehashing feelings, analyzing relationships, playing back conversations, magnifying failures and mistakes—looking for malignancies.

I usually ask such people, "Is all of this self-examination helping you become less depressed?" I can hear the "NO!" chorus as I sit writing this. "Well, then," I suggest, "stop doing it. If it doesn't work, don't do it."

Analyzing until you paralyze is unhealthy and harmful. *Negative feelings foster more negative feelings*. Overanalyzing events and the depressive feelings that arise from them only leads to deeper depression.

Some depressed individuals will protest that they are searching for TRUTH; they are merely trying to be HONEST with themselves. But I've been there, and I found little truth mucking about in a negative, depressed state. What is more, the negative ruminations distort clear thinking. They drive people in the opposite direction of honesty and truth.

You do not need to analyze depression to conquer it! **Repeat this until you've burned it into your brain. It is far better to save the energy that you formerly spent in analysis. Use it instead to create workable solutions for a hopeful future.**

If you find it very hard to quit analyzing (you've been doing it for years, haven't you?), try the following procedure. Whenever your mind starts turning over rocks, go ahead and analyze—but do it with a yellow tablet in your hands. Record every word of your analysis on that tablet. No standing around, idly letting your mind dwell on your troubles. START WRITING.

Next, begin changing your task from analysis of feelings to analysis of how you can outwit your depression. At this point, the only acceptable back-looking analysis is a search for *exceptions* to your depressed feelings (see the method described in the next chapter) or *strengths* you are ignoring. The important thing is to start writing whenever your negative feelings arise.

Remember your school days: when you had to write a paper, you learned a lot more about the subject than when you merely thought about it or memorized it. That's why teachers assign papers. In this case, writing will help you to objectify your feelings and distance yourself from those negative thoughts that overtake you.

Positive thinking

Thought stopping. Worry time. Read, write, and burn. Yellow tablet analysis. Even though each of these methods will lessen the damage caused by negative thoughts, they do not automatically bring about positive ones. You also need to promote positive thinking.

If you have a tendency to minimize your accomplishments, then you might want to perform a daily review of what you have actually achieved, for the time being ignoring what didn't go well.

❏ If you tend to forget your accomplishments, record them on a card that you carry around with you or in your journal.

❏ Periodically read the card or journal entry to keep your eye on what you have accomplished.

❏ Allow yourself to feel justifiably proud of your accomplishments.

The next chapter will describe some additional exercises that can promote positive thinking and actions.

You *can* gain control over thoughts that have become your master through any of the methods described in this chapter. Some of them may be better suited to your particular type of negative thinking; others may simply be better suited to your likes, dislikes, or what you feel least uncomfortable about doing. Don't give up! By working at least one of these methods faithfully, you *will* redirect the unnecessary energy of obsessive thinking toward recovery, toward productive pursuits, toward hope, toward the rest of your life.

TAKE ACTION

Stop those incessant, unwanted thoughts.

✓ Choose one of the methods from this chapter that you are willing to do. Practice it regularly for two weeks.

✓ If you find yourself avoiding worry time, thought stopping, or whatever method you have chosen, put it aside and start over again with one of the other methods.

✓ Record in a notebook the occasions and ways in which you gain more control over your unwanted thoughts. Notice your growing mastery over them. Allow yourself to feel good about it.

FOR THE FAMILY

Don't let one person's negativity poison the family!

✓ When the depression eases up or goes away, your loved one will be more positive again. This is hard to remember when you have been attacked, criticized, cursed, or ignored. So I'll be a broken record and repeat that you must continue with your life as normally as possible.

✓ Is the person ruminating endlessly on problems, fears, guilty feelings, or the like? Don't argue! Keep your cool. You may want to answer negative talk with a calm statement such as "Maybe I can't convince you that you're a good and capable person, but you will *never* convince me that you're no good."

CHAPTER ELEVEN

Think Again:
How to Transform Your Thinking

IN THIS CHAPTER YOU WILL:

✓ Read about a way to overcome the tendency of melancholic persons to focus on what is bad.
✓ Discover that *looking for exceptions* helps us recognize what is going well in our lives; it teaches us to view life more positively and realistically.
✓ Find suggestions for how to begin thinking and talking about your depression in a more hopeful way.
✓ Learn—and begin using—a series of methods that can transform negative thinking.

Can you change how you think? Sounds impossible. A lot of people probably will tell you it can't be done. But if you want to conquer depression, changing how you think is one of the things you need to do.

It is not impossible to transform your thought processes. It's not even very complicated. A number of very doable methods work wonders in changing the negative thinking that can feed depression. This chapter describes twelve of these methods—not that you would use all twelve! For starters, choose one or two that seem right for you. Try them. They will help you begin thinking more positively.

Finding Exceptions

Emma was a lot like many people who struggle with depression. She tended to believe that her problems were embedded in her very being. She didn't even notice those times when a problem was absent (like the hour on a Saturday afternoon when she got up from

Put problems in the past and future goals in the present

Most people speak of their problems in the present tense. It's much more hopeful to use the past tense for what's wrong: "I *slept* away my mornings." "I *avoided* being with people."

At the same time, begin discussing goals and positive behaviors in terms of "when" or "as" instead of "if." For example, say: "What *will occur as* I start to eat in the lunchroom instead of alone at my desk?" (Not: "What *would happen if* I started having lunch with my coworkers?") Assume that you are doing it. Phrase your words hopefully, to express that *you have already started* making the change for the better.

Use concrete, specific words

It is tempting to describe yourself and people close to you in terms of faults. But it's more hopeful to describe specific behaviors instead of making sweeping characterizations.

If my wife tells me, "You're inconsiderate," it's hard for me to know what she wants. If she says, "I'd appreciate it if you would wait for me when you get out of the car instead of walking on ahead of me," I know what I can do. The hopeless goal (reforming my character) changes into an achievable behavior (waiting for Karen to get out of the car).

There is hope. Change is possible when you ask others (and yourself!) for concrete, identifiable behaviors that may need changing.

Talk about improvements instead of problems

One of the biggest obstacles to hopeful conversation is the urge to talk only about what's wrong, to bob and weave from every attempt to discuss solutions. If this description fits, you need to ask yourself: "What will be the very first sign that change is on the way? What will be different when [for example] I start getting up at the same time every morning?"

Try not to focus on that pie-in-the-sky day when everything in your life will be completely as you wish. This makes it hard to notice the first subtle signs of transition and growth. Hopeful conversation points out early hints of improvement.

The change you are undertaking is not a sudden blast; it is more like a gentle breeze on the face. You have to stop for a moment to observe it, and use hopeful words to describe it.

Considering Alternatives

Some people interpret everything that happens in a negative way. Natalie, for example, noticed that her husband, Steve, had become withdrawn and uncommunicative. In her mind she leaped to negative interpretations: he was mad at her, didn't love her anymore, was seeing another woman, was getting ready to leave her, wanted a divorce. The alternative technique was tailor-made for Natalie.

Identify errors in thinking

Using the alternative technique, depressed persons recognize their cognitive errors (see chapter 9). Natalie was *overgeneralizing* and making *unfounded suppositions* when she jumped to conclusions about her husband's quiet, distant behavior.

Identify alternatives

The next step is to come up with new possible explanations for troublesome experiences. Natalie needs to explore alternatives (other than the awful ones) for Steve's behavior. Perhaps he is suffering a fresh wave of grief over the loss of their baby boy fifteen years ago, and doesn't want to add to her troubles by sharing his feelings. He might be up for a promotion at work and wonders if he is adequate to the job. What if he's just worrying about Natalie, but doesn't know how to talk with her about her depression? Natalie needs to get some accurate information, take charge of her feelings, and reach out to Steve.

Once the depressed have substituted negative assumptions with more accurate interpretations of their experiences, they can design alternative strategies for handling life's inevitable problems and ambiguities.

Dis-identification

Instead of looking at their low mood in terms of specific events, circumstances, and choices, many who suffer from depression see it as evidence that they are incompetent, defective, bad.

It's hard not to think this way when you are so low. Therefore it is vital to *separate the person from the depression*. You may *feel* miserable, but it does not follow that you *are* a miserable creature. (That would be *emotional reasoning*.)

Individuals struggling with depression need to separate who they are from what they do, and even from how they feel. By treating the experience of depression as something external, outside their being, they depersonalize it and hold onto their own infinite worth.

Roberto Assagioli (1965, 22) called this method *dis-identification*. The purpose is to separate yourself from your negative emotions, thoughts, or desires. You recognize that you have them, but you don't allow yourself to be defined by them. You come to see yourself as an infinitely precious person, even if what you do isn't always so great.

Relax

The first step in practicing dis-identification begins with relaxation. Find a way to relax. (If necessary, use the relaxation methods described in chapter 7.)

It was all my fault

We'll use Renaldo as an example. I asked him to select a recent disaster from the newspaper. He chose an incident in south Texas when a barge struck a bridge support, causing 160 feet of causeway to collapse and killing a number of motorists. Renaldo's next task was to write a paragraph titled *How I Caused the Collapse of the Causeway*. I asked him to detail every single thing he did or might have done to make that barge smash into the bridge.

At first he couldn't do it, but at my urging he persisted. Finally, Renaldo came up with a long, harebrained story that involved being in the same room with the barge operator at a party in Laredo and oh, if only he had invited the guy to visit him in Fort Worth on that fateful day.

Ridiculous? Of course it is. That's the idea. People who suffer from depression need to discover, in a very graphic way, how pointless it is for them to accept guilt for events they had no part in, and how equally outrageous it is for them to shoulder the blame for events in their own lives over which they have little or no control.

Now it is true that Renaldo hadn't been very assertive in seeking better work for higher pay. He did use a little money for his own pleasure from time to time. But he did not cause the accident that shortened his father's life. It wasn't his fault that his mother chose not to immigrate to the United States after her husband's death. (Renaldo was forlorn, but we who are older can understand that she probably was wise not to leave the support of her long-time friends and neighbors.)

I should be able to control . . .

What about a parent, say a father, who feels he has failed his children because they tattoo their bodies, put rings in their noses, and dye their hair yellow-green? I might suggest: "In the coming week, your job is to help your son [whose musical appreciation is limited to hip-hop] to develop a taste for early classical music. I want you to try every possible way to get him to adore Pachelbel. By the end of the week, he will have taken up the hammered dulcimer and be sewing his costume for next year's Renaissance Festival."

Not going to happen. Dad is the last person on earth who can expand his son's musical universe.

This exercise would have been useful for the mother (see chapter 9) who was upset because her daughter was not accepted in her first college of choice. Trying to achieve a task that is so obviously unattainable leads us to reflect on what we can and cannot control.

You may want to invent your own guilt-overload tasks. They aren't likely to change your situation, but they can change how you think about it. They can help you to discern what is and isn't controllable in your real, flesh-and-blood world.

Lectio Divina—Sacred Reading

For religious people, depression can be a spiritual wasteland. Not only does it affect oneself and one's relationships, but it also can have an effect on one's relationship with God. It is as if God is absent.

Thankfully, there are ways to involve your spiritual life as you overcome your depression. *Lectio divina*, a centuries-old method of meditative prayer, is one of them. (I have covered several other spiritual disciplines in greater detail elsewhere [Stone 1994].)

Lectio divina, in short, is a way to meditate on scripture. (For a more complete introduction to *Lectio divina*, I recommend Michael Casey's book *Sacred Reading*, 1995.) It comes out of the ancient tradition of spiritual direction, in which seekers consult with spiritual advisors to enrich their inner life and their relationship with God.

What can **Lectio divina** do for you? It can lead you to become less obsessed with your own problems. It can allow you to center on ultimate meaning—beyond yourself, beyond unhappy circumstances. It offers a chance to develop and extend your relationship to God.

> *A caution:* **Those who suffer from depression need to be careful not to use scripture, prayer, meditation, and contemplation as another excuse to retreat from the world around them.**

The following simple steps can get you started in the use of *Lectio divina.*

Quiet down

First you need to quiet yourself, perhaps by way of relaxation exercises, imaging, or regularized breathing (see chapter 7). For those who already are fairly relaxed, a breathing exercise is a good way to begin. Close your eyes and simply count your breaths, or mentally say, "I am," as you inhale and "calm" (or "relaxed") as you exhale.

Read

Next, slowly read a short passage from the Bible or other sacred text several times over. The Psalms are a good place to start. When reading a selection, take time to reflect on the passage and listen for meanings. The process should not be forced; it is important to stay in a patient, receptive mode. Don't expect immediate, earthshaking revelations.

Breathe and meditate

In the final step, close your eyes and again become aware of your breathing. Mentally repeat phrases from the selection you have read and coordinate it with your breathing. Using Psalm 23 (NEB) as an example:

❑ Remove the nozzle from the pump and lift the lever.

❑ Press the REGULAR fuel selection button.

❑ Push the nozzle into your gas tank, squeeze the handle, and flip down the little ridged metal piece that locks it in place so the gas will flow automatically.

❑ Put your credit card back in your wallet.

❑ When you hear the gas pump click off, remove it from the car (lift the nozzle so gas won't drip on the paint).

❑ Lower the lever and replace the nozzle.

❑ Screw the gas cap back on and close the cover.

❑ Tear off the receipt.

❑ Get in your car. Place the receipt in the ashtray.

❑ Put on your seat belt.

❑ Put your key in the ignition. Turn it clockwise to start the engine.

❑ Put the transmission in DRIVE.

❑ Check all of your mirrors, then slowly pull away from the pumps and out of the gas station.

This flowchart made me nostalgic for the days when you could just roll into a gas station and say, "Fill 'er up!" Roger was amazed at the number of actions that he had to perform correctly and in sequence in order to fill his tank with gas. (To save space, I left out the part where he washes his windshield and checks his oil!) Roger *almost* enjoyed doing this (though he wasn't ready to admit it).

Why not try this exercise right now? It's interesting—some people think it's fun. You will be amazed at your overlooked capabilities. Be careful not to skip steps; you won't get any gas if you forget to push the fuel selection button.

Chart your depression

Once you have documented how to tie your shoes, iron a shirt, or fill your tank with gas, it is time for step two: *Make a flowchart of how you get depressed.*

Think of a recent event that led you deeper into depression. Be very specific and note each step that you took that led to the episode. Be sure to include how you handled ambiguous information (e.g., your girlfriend/mother/daughter/wife didn't call you as she usually does).

Please take this task very seriously. Try to tease out every tiny step that leads to the depressive tailspin. Ask a close friend or family member—someone who will take this seriously without being over-critical—to look over your chart and add forgotten steps.

The depression flowchart simply reverses the order of the flowchart for assembling a piece of furniture: you learn how you get depressed and therefore what *not* to do. Now you can design an alternative way of responding to life's frustrations and uncertainties.

Roger's gas-pumping flowchart broke his vicious circle so he could form a more realistic picture of his abilities. This gave him enough confidence to take other actions against his melancholia. His depression flowchart helped him to examine (and replace) the self-defeating thoughts and actions that led to his dark mood.

The Inner Critic

What's that little voice inside your head, telling you terrible things about yourself? It's your inner critic!

In thirty-five years of counseling, I have noticed that depressed people are very attentive to this malicious voice—they pay more attention to it than to God, loved ones, or anyone else.

People who are not particularly depressed may listen momentarily to those fault-finding inner voices. They quickly assess whether the criticism has any validity, ignore it or take care of it, and move on with life. In contrast, the depressed tend to believe whatever their inner critic has to say.

Whoa. Have you ever considered laughing at your inner critic? Refuting its bad logic? Making fun of it? The following exercise will do just that (Yapko 1996). Try to follow along with these three steps:

1. Close your eyes and allow your inner critic to talk to you for a minute or so. Listen to what it is saying and be aware of what you feel.

2. Next think of a funny voice (Daffy Duck, Ross Perot, Mickey Mouse). Give this voice to your inner critic. Let it continue talking to you. The result is an *auditory shift*. The inner critic is not saying anything different; only its voice has changed.

I might say to such people, "*I'm thankful you don't treat others like you treat yourself. If you did, you would be very cruel. I would like to see you treat yourself with the same dignity, respect, and compassion that you treat others.*"

If you beat up on yourself, read these sentences out loud several times. Then consider ways in which you can treat yourself with the dignity and respect you would give to others. Forgive yourself for past mistakes—you probably were doing the best you could with the information you had. After all, you are an infinitely worthy person. You deserve better.

Faulty thinking can perpetuate despair, but change is possible. Use some of the methods that help people alter the way they think, and thus bring your depression under greater control.

The goal of these methods is not necessarily to eradicate depression (a daunting, perhaps even impossible task) but to manage it, confine it, and limit its impact on your life so that you can have a fruitful, satisfying existence.

You can learn to treat yourself with consideration and kindness. Even relapses of depression lose their terror once you realize how to replace negative thoughts with positive thinking. Renewed life lies before you—a life filled with dangers, to be sure, but also with meaning and purpose.

TAKE ACTION

Transform your thinking.

This chapter has discussed a dozen ways to change your thinking so it will be more positive and less depressing. Choose one of the methods and put it into practice for a few days, a week, or two weeks if you can think that far down the road. Notice ways in which you feel better as you change how you think. You might want to take note in your journal.

Here are the twelve methods again:

1. Finding Exceptions: What is going on when my problem is absent or not so bad?
2. Hopeful Conversation: What word choices will help me think more positively?
3. Alternatives: What are some neutral or positive explanations for this event? What facts do I need before making conclusions?
4. Dis-Identificaton: I am not my problems. My depression is not me.
5. Reassigning Blame: I'm not at fault for things I couldn't control. Who or what is really to blame?
6. Guilt Overload: By carrying my self-blaming to ridiculous extremes, maybe I can see how useless it is.
7. *Lectio Divina:* I can create a meditative prayer out of a scripture passage.
8. Depression Flowchart: What do I do well, and how do I do it? What are my steps to depression, and how can I reverse the process?
9. Inner Critic: Why not make fun of my mean, fault-finding inner voice?
10. Options: What might other people do in my predicament? I need to give myself more freedom of choice.
11. Resignation: I will accept what cannot be changed and develop realistic, hopeful goals.
12. Be Kind to a Depressed Person: I will treat myself with the respect and dignity that all people deserve.

FOR THE FAMILY

Thinking differently about the depression can help family members. For example:

✓ Look for exceptions. It is easy to think the depressed family member is miserable 24/7, but in fact, few depressed people are low every hour of every day. Look for times when the person is less depressed. Examine what's going on. Find ways to make those better times happen more often.

✓ Try to speak to the depressed person as well as to yourself in more hopeful conversation.

✓ Rename the depression.

✓ Focus more on future goals than a troubled past.

✓ Dis-identification, Resignation, and Options may also work for you.

✓ From this chapter, choose one method that appeals to you. Put it into practice for a month. If it helps, do more of it; if not, try another one.

CHAPTER TWELVE

Journey of a Thousand Miles: The Behavioral Face of Depression

IN THIS CHAPTER YOU WILL:

✓ Grasp the good news that depression is more a matter of *behavior* than feeling, and learn that to conquer depression is to act differently.

✓ Consider that taking action calls for resources, and discover what resources you already have—and what new resources you might develop—for tackling depression.

✓ Discover one of the first actions that can decrease the effects of depression: start creating a new vision for what your life will be like when you are not depressed.

✓ Learn two simple methods—questions, really—that can help you fashion a vision for a better life to come: the *future question* and the *miracle question.*

✓ Recognize that you can make your realistic dreams come true, and find a step-by-step, doable way to bring about your new vision for the future.

Depression has both a physiological face and a cognitive aspect. But the problem does not lie only in misfiring neurotransmitters and flawed thinking; it's also a matter of behavior. You can't get around it: to conquer depression is to act differently.

Roger, who made the flow chart for putting gas in his car (chapter 11), most likely had a physiological predisposition to depression, and we know he struggled with negative thought processes. In fact, he had always tended towards a pessimistic self-image. But after he lost his job, he came to see himself as incompetent, irresponsible, stupid, and hopeless. He believed that failure was his permanent lot, and viewed himself and his abilities (or lack of abilities) through that lens.

Behaviorally, what did Roger do? He caved in. Certain that he would fail, he stopped attempting to do important tasks in his life. By not trying, he accomplished less and thus thought even less of himself.

In reality, people rarely are depressed all the time. Even the most severe depression lifts somewhat for days or portions of days. (Roger wasn't noticeably depressed, for example, while he was putting gas in his car.)

Taking action calls for resources. The first step in a journey toward freedom from depression is to find out accurately what skills and abilities can be summoned to tackle the problem.

Recognize Strengths

Every individual possesses certain abilities, skills, and strengths. In the midst of depression, however, you probably do not recognize your inner resources. Or perhaps you dismiss them as false, trivial, or accidental. You will have more success at combating depression if you recognize and act upon your strengths, rely upon your gifts, and use your best resources.

In a sense, those suffering with depression sometimes act like pathologists looking for disease. Instead of creating a new vision for the future, they focus on what is going wrong now or has failed in the past. They view the bad things that have happened to them as a predetermined, changeless pattern. A better perspective is to think of your melancholia as a sign, or a call for action. *Change lanes!*

Depression can give rise to new action and redirection. Life does not have to be hopeless. But you may need different strategies and skills for dealing with certain areas of your life, and you need to remember and use the strengths you already have. Even a modest rise in the way you esteem yourself and your abilities will give you renewed strength to take action.

Behaviors can change feelings faster than feelings can change behaviors.
**Write this on a card and stick it on your refrigerator.
Enlarge it, frame it, hang it over your desk.**

Educators recognize this principle. They know that the surest way to bring about positive self-esteem in children is not to praise, reward, or be nice to them (all of which are good), and certainly not to berate or punish them, but to help them *achieve success at their tasks.* Success at doing something raises self-esteem, which ensures greater success at doing the next thing.

Similarly, one of the quickest ways to feel better about yourself is to take actions that capture some of your forgotten strengths. Unlike money in the bank, you have to use your inner resources to know you have them. By doing so you move from pathology, problems, and excuses to competence, strengths, and solutions.

TAKE ACTION

Discover and use your strengths.

✓ Take out your journal or notebook and make a list of your strengths.

✓ *Be very specific.* (For example: I am very friendly and greet everyone when they first arrive at work; I am a detail person and can balance any set of financial books; I offer to help out my older neighbors.)

✓ Next, take a few actions that use some of these strengths. If you were friendly before this melancholy took over, go back to greeting everyone when they arrive for work. If you help out your elderly neighbors, get up out of your chair, pick up the phone or walk next door, and offer to do a specific task for one of them.

✓ You have to use these inner resources to know you have them. Use it or lose it.

Form a Vision for the Future

One of the first actions that can decrease the effects of depression is to start creating a new vision for what your life might be like when you are not depressed. It's all too easy to stay frozen in the unchangeable past and therefore perceive little or no freedom in the present and future. Establishing future goals (discussed later in this chapter) can open up a vision for what the future will be like when depression no longer dominates.

Two simple methods—questions, really—can help you fashion a vision for the future. The purpose of both is to help you refocus and think about the future in a positive, hopeful way.

The future question

Answer this question: *"How do I want my life to be different three months from now"* (Stone 1998)?

Be very specific and concrete.

❑ List in detail what you would like to see in your home, work, and leisure existence.

❑ This is not a fantasy. Keep in mind your financial situation, family obligations, and job.

- ❑ Ignore the voice in your head that tells you why you can't do this or that.

- ❑ Who will you spend time with?

- ❑ What new activities will you take on?

- ❑ Be positive; direct your efforts at what you *will* be doing, thinking, and so forth.

For example: "I will sign up for a computer class so that I can get a better job in the comptroller's office." "I will join Al-Anon and learn how to live with my husband's drinking." "I will join choir at church to help me get out and interact with people." "I will return to the aerobics class and get myself back in shape."

The miracle question

Suppose that I woke up tomorrow morning and my problem was magically gone—how would I know? If by magic the problem vanished overnight, what would be different in my life? How would my family or friends know? How would they say that I had changed (de Shazer 1988, 5; Stone 1998)?

This is the miracle question. Answer it. Again, be very specific. Think about what kind of life you will be leading when this miracle occurs and your life is no longer dominated by depression.

Resist the voice in your head that tells you that miracles never happen, that magic doesn't exist.

As with the future question, state everything in positive terms:

- ❑ What are your first thoughts when you get out of bed?

- ❑ Will you have a different kind of breakfast?

- ❑ Are you dressing or fixing your hair differently?

- ❑ Are you starting a new project?

- ❑ How will you talk differently to your wife (husband, children, colleagues at work, friends, etc.)?

- ❑ What words will you say?

The future question and the miracle question create hope by encouraging us not only to conceive a new future, but also to develop specific objectives that can move us toward that future.

The following paragraphs offer a way to go about creating that new future, not just envisioning it, but making it *happen*.

I want you to begin having that future today.

TAKE ACTION

Form a vision for the future.

✓ Construct a realistic vision of what you want the future to be like when depression no longer holds so much control over you.

✓ Ask yourself either the miracle question or the future question discussed above.

✓ It may help to open a notebook or turn on your computer and start recording your answers. Keep adding to your notes over the next few days.

Focus on Results

For years I have been fascinated with very successful people. How can they accomplish so many things and keep on smiling? I have talked to some about how they do it, and many of them don't have a clue. They seem to do it intuitively. Watch them, though, and you will see a pattern.

Here are some things I have observed about the way many successful people operate. Can you put some of these ideas into practice in your life?

Planning

My wife and I sometimes travel with two wonderful friends, Bob and Jon Leah. It's our tradition on these trips to sit down to a big breakfast every morning. As plates are cleared and napkins folded, Bob announces brightly: "We gotta have a plan." This is the time to check the skies, see how everyone's feeling, spread out a map, establish meeting places if we get separated, and modify the long-range plan to suit our wishes for the day.

Gotta have a plan. Everybody can successfully make changes and bring about hopeful goals, but it calls for planning. You need to know where you're going *(goals)*, how you're going to get there *(method)*, and what specific steps you will take toward achieving your goals *(actions)*. All three elements of good planning—goals, method, and actions—are necessary.

I fear that many people in the grips of depression don't have a plan at all. If they have goals, they often state them vaguely. They may have little sense of the steps required to achieve the goals. Sometimes they will try to fix several problems all at once (kind of like trying to go to Acapulco, Guadalajara, and Mexico City all in the same day). Inevitably this fails, and so they get stuck in neutral. It's not surprising if they feel they'll never accomplish anything.

This is pretty much where we first met Roger. After he had made the artistic flowcharts that I described in chapter 12, he began to acknowledge that he did have a number of abilities and skills. Some of them might even be useful in managing his melancholia. But where did he want to go, exactly? How would he go about getting there? What would he do if he came to roadblocks or detours? Clearly, Roger needed a plan.

Gotta have a plan. You need to strategize the steps necessary for achieving your vision for a better future. For example, you might watch and talk with successful people to learn how they set and reach their goals. ("Success" does not mean fame and riches. An auto mechanic who fixes your car the first time, doesn't get grease on the seat, and reads to his kids at night is a successful person.)

Keep in mind that you will have to modify the role models' procedures to fit your own personality and situation in life. Also remember that you must begin at the beginning. You are learning how to do something that they have been doing for many years, perhaps all their lives. You can hardly expect to be as successful as they are, not at first. But you will progress.

A model for problem solving

The purpose of any problem-solving model is to make realistic dreams come true. Successful attorneys and business people manage effectively because they set goals and follow strategies for putting their goals into action. Their pattern for problem solving and achievement may be either conscious or intuitive; either way, it's in place and in use.

Why reinvent the wheel? It's fine to adopt someone else's problem-solving model, such as the one presented below. This is not the only model around, but it has worked for me and for a number of counselees I have seen over the years. Of course, you will have to modify it to suit your own personality and interests.

It's a start. In the absence of your own system, follow this one. It will direct your wishes and hopes into action so they will actually happen!

I call it the GRACE model. GRACE is an acronym for the five tasks of addressing a problem, envisioning a future, and beginning to bring that future into action:

Goals
Resources
Alternatives
Commitment to action
Evaluation

Goals

Think of the old saying, "The journey of a thousand miles begins with a single step." Pinpoint target goals that you can achieve in a very short period of time, and determine how you will reach them. Your first goal should be something you know you can (and will) do.

What if you face an assortment of problems? You need to choose just one goal as the highest priority and work to achieve it. Narrowing the focus to a single, achievable goal increases the likelihood that change will occur.

Questions that lead you to claim a new vision of the future (such as the miracle question or future question discussed above) will help you identify specific ways in which your life will be different.

Looking for exceptions to problems (see chapter 11) is another way to find a direction—not an entirely new direction, but one that already has worked for you.

Good goals have at least seven key elements (Berg 1991):

❑ They must be considered *important*. If you don't think a goal is important, you probably will not accomplish it.

❑ They should describe the desired change in *specific* action terms. They are measurable; exactly how will you know when you have achieved a particular goal?

❑ Goals are best kept *small*—not "I'll go to college and graduate," but "This afternoon I will drive to the nearest community college and request an application and catalog of courses."

❑ They need to be understood as the *infancy of a new future vision*. Not everything can be accomplished immediately. Goals chart out the first actions toward a (possibly new) direction that you want to take.

❑ Goals must be *realistic and doable within a short time* (hours, days, possibly weeks—not years or decades).

❑ Goals should involve *effort*. We learn and progress best when we push ourselves just enough to feel the exertion, but not so hard that we fail or give up in dismay. It's a good thing to have to work for your success.

❑ Goals should be stated *positively* and should describe the *presence of something good* rather than the absence of something bad. For a couple that fight a lot, their stated goal should not be to stop fighting, but to (for example) do the dishes together or speak politely to each other.

Here is a good example of goal setting. Fada is feeling pretty low. Her last child married an Air Force pilot and is stationed in Turkey, leaving a void in the house and in Fada's life. Her long-term goal is to fill that void. A specific, short-term goal might be to begin gathering information about starting up the Internet business that she often talked about, but never had time to do.

This goal uses all seven key elements. It is important, specific, small, and short-term (with an eye to the long-range result). It requires effort. It is stated positively and describes the presence of something good rather than the absence of something bad. (Fada doesn't say: "My goal is to quit walking through the empty bedrooms and weeping.") Even if her fledgling business doesn't take off, Fada has a good chance of success at finding the meaning she seeks.

Resources

By now you may already have jotted down some good goals. Your next step is to take stock of the resources you have in store for working toward these goals.

Internal resources are your inner strengths and skills, coping methods, and successful past experiences with problem solving. Everyone has gone through problems in life, and everyone has negotiated at least some of them successfully. Bring those to mind. Write them down.

(If you have trouble doing this, go back to chapter 13. Until he completed the flow-chart exercises, Roger would not have been able to catalog his internal resources because he didn't believe he had any.)

External resources are found in your environment—church, community groups and agencies, family and friends, schools, money and assets, and so forth. These resources offer much in the way of advice, assistance, moral support, and gratification as you resolve difficult situations. List these as well.

Your inventory should include how you might use these resources, and what difficulties you might encounter when you call upon them.

Alternatives

After establishing goals and assessing resources, it's time to brainstorm. What are some possible actions for reaching a solution? List them *all* on a piece of paper—the wacky and dubious as well as the plausible and promising. If you are willing, let family members or friends help you; the more courses of action you can put on your list, the better. (But don't forget, it's best that most of the ideas come from you—after all, you're the one who's taking action, not your family!)

Now start narrowing down your brainstorm list. Weed out inappropriate items. Since more than one course of action may achieve the same goal, you will want to consider your personal values as you sift through the possibilities. Your work schedule, family obligations, and finances may rule out some of the choices.

Next you need to evaluate the remaining courses of action. How effectively will each alternative contribute to your goal? The best choice may be a combination of two or more actions; therefore no single idea should be dismissed too quickly.

Committing to action

When you've narrowed the list of alternatives to one or a few that you think will have a high chance of success, it's time to make a firm commitment. If possible, break the action down into even smaller steps that are concrete, measurable, and easy to attain.

Then step out on your chosen course.

Taking action is essential. However, if at this point you find yourself resisting action for a variety of reasons, don't worry. You are not the only one. There is still hope. Chapter 15 will provide you with several methods to ensure that you accomplish your goals—ways to get going and ways to keep going, ways to make your future vision a reality.

Evaluation

As you set goals and work toward them, you continue to evaluate them, even if you don't notice that you're doing it. (*I'm too embarrassed to ask that question, so I'll get my friend to ask it while I listen. I can't bring myself to make this phone call, so today I'll just look up the number and write out what I want to say. Filling out one online job application made me feel more hopeful, so tomorrow I'll do three.*)

Once you've actually started taking action, make a conscious effort to analyze and evaluate how it's going. At the end of a day or a week, sit down and review what you have done. What worked? What didn't? Why? What changes do you need to make in your plan?

When your review shows progress, you feel encouraged to continue. When it shows need for more progress (and it will, believe me), resist the urge to throw the whole plan overboard. Instead, refine and modify either the goal or the course of action.

Your behavioral approach to conquering depression needs to follow a systematic plan. But your plan is not inscribed in stone. It's more organic, like a rosebush that requires nourishment and pruning in order to grow and blossom. As you put your plan into action, you will have to be flexible and adaptable, refining and modifying at each step along the way.

Any positive behavioral change that you make is a good beginning. Like the tiniest green shoot on a plant you thought had died, it can lead to hope's return.

FOR THE FAMILY

Do something different.

Let's say you have tried several of the suggestions in the FOR THE FAMILY boxes. Some have worked very well, some have worked moderately well. Maybe some of them have bombed.

Did you throw up your hands in disgust or frustration? Did you want to give up?

Here is another approach. Let's say your husband comes home drunk again. No matter how many times you have helped him out of his clothes and into bed, no matter how many times you have pointed out that his drinking is not good for him, he continues to do it. Not every day, mind you, but enough to cause problems at home.

Face it: what you have been doing isn't working. Why continue doing it? DO SOMETHING DIFFERENT!

✓ Ahead of time, plan what you will do *differently*, then resolve to do it.
✓ For example, next time hubby walks in the door inebriated, put on you best gown and start singing opera tunes. Go bowling. Go out for a meal with your best friend. Knit. Jog. Practice your Japanese.
✓ Just so it's different.

You will be surprised how easily you can begin to break the old cycle when you merely give up what isn't working and try something new.

CHAPTER THIRTEEN

Doing What Needs to Be Done

IN THIS CHAPTER YOU WILL:

✓ Observe that depression can be a vicious spiral in which a reduction in constructive activities can lead to depressed feelings, which lead to decreased interest in activities that might have positive outcomes, which leads to fewer positive outcomes, and thus to even greater depression.

✓ Note, also, that it is not always easy to become active—but when you do, you begin to feel at least slightly better.

✓ Apply an important educational principle to the task of overcoming depression: when the work is too hard for the students' level, they will fail, but when the work is too easy, they will not learn anything new.

✓ Understand that, if you are a victim, it is hard *not* to be depressed.

✓ Learn how to switch from being a victim to being a survivor.

✓ Realize that change occurs when people exercise mastery over their environment, and that to succeed in defeating depression, you need to distinguish between what you can (and should) control and what you cannot (or should not try to) control, then invest your energies appropriately.

Have you ever listened to "A Prairie Home Companion" on Public Radio? After thirty-five years, this entertaining and often wise radio variety show is still on the air. It's hosted by Garrison Keillor (one of America's great storytellers) and sponsored by Powdermilk Biscuits, "tasty and expeditious," those flaky but substantial melt-in-your-mouth morsels that "give you the strength to get up and do what needs to be done."

Perhaps you already know what needs to be done. You need to get up and clean the house. You need to get out of the house. You need to spend time with friends. You need to start exercising, improve your diet, give up caffeine, lose weight, get a job, weed the garden, do your taxes, tackle the heap of bills on your desk. Problem is, you just don't have the strength. The "do" list grows longer and longer. You feel guiltier, lower, hopeless, helpless.

Oh, wouldn't you like some Powdermilk Biscuits right now? They may be a fiction of Garrison Keillor's imagination, but in a way they do exist. Keillor strikes a familiar nerve— that uncomfortable no-person's-land between what we ought to do and our lethargy. We need something—anything—to give us strength to carry on.

Getting Active

Melancholia is a vicious spiral. Any reduction in constructive activities can lead to depressed feelings; these feelings lead to decreased interest in activities that might have positive outcomes, which leads to fewer positive outcomes, and thus to even greater depression. And so on and so on and so on.

Reversing the downward spiral

Improved performance in almost any activity leads to improved self-assessment. It increases the motivation to do even more, which leads to improved performance, and so on. Clearly, one way for depressed individuals to get going is to get active—whether they feel like it or not.

The law of inertia

When Karen, my gifted wife, was a teenager with a B average, it was obvious that she was not living up to her potential. Her father took her aside in his study and told her about the law of inertia. She learned it from him before she learned it in science class: *a body in motion tends to remain in motion, and a body at rest tends to remain at rest.* He let her know that she was particularly subject to this physical law, and that she always needed to put herself in motion so that she would not waste her gifts.

Still, on occasion, Karen struggles with this law. Then she can hear her father's words. When she has an overwhelming task at hand, she sometimes says to herself: I'll just get out the files. Or, I'll just stir the paint and try out the color on this wall. I'll clean up three dirty dishes. I'll put away five items that I left sitting on the counter. I'll just pay one bill and put it in the mail.

What do you think happens when she does these little steps? It's almost obvious. Having taken the first step, she will finish the project, or at least get a big chunk of it out of the way. The counter is clean. The dishes are done. At least one wall is painted. The bills are paid, the filing done.

Tricking yourself

Can you trick yourself to get going? Like Karen, can you tell yourself, "I don't have to do it all—I'll just do this one little bit?" Walk around the block, as a first step toward an exercise program? Write a short note to a friend who you can't quite bring yourself to call on the telephone? Open *all* of your mail (even those ominous-looking envelopes) without promising necessarily to do something about all of it? Start boiling water, even if you haven't the faintest idea what you're going to cook?

These little tricks may help you to get up and do what needs to be done. In many ways, depression is a disease of inertia. If you can't drag yourself out of bed in the morning, try—in the smallest, least threatening way—to put the positive side of the law of inertia to work for you (a body in motion tends to stay in motion).

This chapter will discuss how you can get active. It also will explore some of the things you need to watch out for—experiences that can lull you back to inactivity—and tips for moving onward. Remember: *A body in motion tends to remain in motion.*

Passivity and inaction are major obstacles for those who suffer depression. It is not always an easy task to become active—but when you do, you begin to feel at least slightly better.

Sometimes people who feel depressed wait until they have enough motivation to act. This is a big mistake. Like would-be artists waiting for inspiration before taking brush to canvas, many of them assume that they must feel like doing something before they can do it. As a result, they produce little or nothing.

Studies of successful people show that they work whether they feel inspired or not. In fact, many productive people report that they rarely experience inspiration before they begin a task. Their *motivation arises out of doing it.*

Allow me to repeat: Not only does a body at rest tend to remain at rest; a body in motion tends to remain in motion. It is convenient to feel like doing the right thing, but frequently it's not realistic. If you are depressed, acting according to your depressed feelings usually leads to inactivity. Instead, you need (in the words of Garrison Keillor) to "get up and do what needs to be done"—again, *whether you feel like it or not.*

Scaffolding: Improving at a Realistic Pace

An important educational principle goes something like this: when the work is too hard for the students' level, they will fail. When the work is too easy, they will not learn anything new.

Building on existing skills

This principle underlies the idea of *scaffolding,* or building on top of previous knowledge and skills. What do you need to grow, learn, improve, or make progress—whether in managing your depression or in any other area of your life? You need a doable challenge.

First, undertake an activity that *you can achieve.* It must involve some skills or knowledge that you already possess. If a task is beyond your understanding or ability, you cannot learn from it. Imagine, for example, giving a thousand-piece jigsaw puzzle to six-year-old

Lucy and challenging her to finish it by bedtime tomorrow. She can't learn from it because it's beyond her ability; the task will end in frustration, failure, and probably in tears.

But you also need a task that *stretches your present skills* and knowledge if you are to learn from it. Now picture Lucy working a nine-piece, preschool level puzzle. She won't learn a thing by doing it, because she has already mastered it. A hundred-piece puzzle, with Mom or Dad helping so she can observe the procedure, might be appropriate scaffolding at Lucy's level. She can finish it, with help, but she will have to push herself and learn new skills.

Setting realistic goals

What tasks have you set before yourself? What are your goals? Are they realistic? Are they challenging?

TOO LOW: I'm always going to be depressed, so I'll just stay here in bed and watch television. Okay, I'll get out of bed and do something, but I'm afraid of crowds so I'll just make a batch of oatmeal cookies. I'll take a course online rather than at the community college, because I might make a fool of myself in class. I will get out of retail sales and ask for a transfer to the warehouse; back there no one will care if I don't smile and my hair is stringy.

TOO HIGH: I never want to feel sad or low again. I should tutor reading to poor children three days a week. I'll always be kind and loving to my family. I will never be afraid. I should feel good every day. I'll open up a restaurant and make a lot of money. I will run a marathon and win a trophy in my age category. I'm going to be perfectly organized like my friend Carolyn. I want to write a best-selling novel.

The day may come when you *can* achieve some of these too-high goals. That day is not today. What *can* you accomplish? Even if it is a little on the easy side, go ahead and set it as a goal for tomorrow. Do it. Then make sure that the following day's goal is a little more challenging.

Victims Are Ripe for Depression

Have you been abused—physically, verbally, or emotionally? Has someone used you? Do you have a cruel spouse (mother, boss, sibling) who makes your life miserable? Do rainy days get you down (and you live in Seattle or London)? Were you overlooked for a promotion, snubbed by a neighbor, cheated by a home repair company, targeted by the tax assessor? Do you suffer from bigotry, unfairness, dirty dealing, or just plain bad luck? Is all of this out of your control?

It is hard not to be depressed, if this is true. Why? Not because all of these people have done bad things to you, surprisingly enough. Countless people encounter similar injustices without necessarily suffering from melancholia. One of the reasons for your despair is not what has been done to you, but *your helplessness in the face of it*. If you are a victim, it's hard not to be depressed.

Victims have no control over their pain. They are the acted-upon rather than the actors. Some victims are more interested in blaming than changing. These people may well have been victimized as children, when they were genuinely helpless. The problem is, they keep on acting like victims even as they grow older and accumulate knowledge, experience, and resources that they could use to improve their lives.

It may be true that others have victimized you. Eddie was victimized as a child. What was done to Eddie and the other Eddies I have met is serious and hard to overcome. I wish it had not happened.

Eddie's mother had a drinking problem. When he was a child, she either ignored him or beat him with a belt. He had to cobble together his own meals. A kind neighbor sometimes cleaned his wounds and fed him. (Today, of course, the kind neighbor would have to call Child Protective Services.) One day when Eddie was fourteen, his mother jumped on the back of some guy's motorcycle and disappeared down the road. It was two weeks before anyone noticed that he was on his own.

Eddie had a pretty rough start in life. However, if in adulthood he was to continue acting helpless and resist steps toward improving his life, he has *victimized himself*. That is not to minimize what has happened to him; nevertheless, Eddie would become the present-day victimizer of Eddie.

If you persist in blaming yourself for every problem, if you describe yourself in global and permanent terms ("I am useless, I'm hopelessly irresponsible, I can't do anything right"), *you are the victimizer and the victim*. Now you are doing it to yourself. It's important to remember that you were taught to think like this. *You have learned to be helpless* (more about that later).

Surprisingly, Eddie did not learn to be helpless. He couldn't do anything about his beatings and the verbal abuse his mother dished out, but he taught himself self-reliance. He fixed things, invented things; later on he supported his kids. His marriage was not all that bad. Okay, maybe Eddie didn't have the greatest opinion of himself. He probably experienced mild depression. But he wasn't helpless and he didn't consider himself a victim. When someone brought up the subject of his mother, he would always say, "I just figure she was doing the best she could." That attitude made it a lot easier for Eddie (finally, in his fifties) to take action and improve his emotional well-being.

Certainly there are plenty of outside pressures that encourage you to feel victimized. A few liberation movements, in their good and important efforts to gain equal treatment for all people, have occasionally (and unintentionally) spawned small but vocal fringe groups that take a combative victim stance. Some of these folks would rather place the burden for change upon the oppressor, rather than give their followers tools to gain control of their own futures and take responsibility for positive change. When asked, "Do you want to be right, or do you want to have a better life?" their response would be: "I want to be right."

Don't get me wrong—the injustice is real. But how you interpret and respond to the injustice is up to you. If you believe you are helpless to improve your situation, plenty of people out there will go along with you. But if you learned to be a victim, isn't it also possible that you can learn to take back control of your life? If you have learned to blame, can't you also learn to accept responsibility?

I Have It under Control

Change occurs when people exercise mastery over their environment. Successful people are not afraid to use their power. To succeed in overcoming depression, you need to distinguish between what you can (and should) control and what you cannot (or should not try to) control. Then you need to invest your energies appropriately. Do what you can and let go of the rest.

Isn't this the meaning of the Serenity Prayer used in Alcoholics Anonymous and other twelve-step groups? "God grant me the serenity to accept the things I cannot change, the courage to change the things I can, and the wisdom to know the difference"?

Depression can turn things "bass-ackwards" (as Eddie put it). Maybe you try to change things that are not yours to change, or you become a victim and do not even try to change things that are within your power.

If you have experienced depression, it is vital to make a realistic assessment of your situation, determine what you can and cannot control, and invest your efforts in whatever you can control. At the same time, you need to release control in those situations that are beyond your power to manage.

Wanting control is not wrong or neurotic. It means that you wish to be successful, to accomplish something. Change occurs because we take control of something. The need to control is fundamental to our lives as human beings.

Take Sarah, for example. She drank more than she should have at a graduation party, and afterward was filled with embarrassment and remorse. Her friend Billie chided her, "You need to get into therapy and deal with your control issues." Sarah thought about it for a minute, then replied, "Wouldn't it just be easier to not drink too much?"

Writing a book is a control-friendly situation. I have to seize ideas, then fashion them into a semblance of order and coherence for the book to have value—let alone get published.

When I try to get my wife to do what I want her to do, it is a control-unfriendly situation. Although I can negotiate vigorously for the change I want (and believe me, I do), I also need to respect her wishes. I cannot control her if she chooses not to be controlled.

Under-control and over-control

Those who suffer from depression have a tendency to either overcontrol or under-control their environment. Undercontrol is more common; it's that old helpless victim mind-set.

Psychologist Martin Seligman (1973, 1974, 1983) performed several studies on the subject of learned helplessness. Volunteers received an uncomfortable stimulus (such as a minor shock) that they could not control; no matter what they tried to do, they could not escape it. Later, the environment was changed so that they could escape the unpleasant stimulus, but the participants no longer tried to escape. They had learned to be helpless. Seligman believes that those suffering from depression act like the subjects of his experiment; they stop trying to control their lives in a favorable way. They feel, and therefore become, helpless and hopeless.

At first Roger (chapters 11 and 12) found it difficult to exercise control or take on activities that would help him manage his depression. He was an undercontroller. He wouldn't apply for a job, didn't try to make love, gave up doing tasks around the house. In short, he knuckled under.

Not all depressed people are undercontrolling victims. Overcontrollers also lack "the wisdom to know the difference" between what they can and cannot manage. They try to master situations that are out of their range. They attempt to change things that are not within their power. They fail, of course. What a perfect reason to slide into depression!

Depression does not only happen to the marginally gifted. Given its physiological components, it can strike randomly at a wide assortment of personalities. Some spectacularly competent people, highly successful in their work, experience depression related to over-control.

High achievers frequently determine their worth by what they do. They expect nothing short of excellence in every area of their lives. No matter how successful they are in one realm, if they fail in another they can become miserable, depressed, and despondent.

It is hazardous for the depression-prone to become involved in activities or events over which they have little control:

❑ Want to volunteer for a public television fund-raiser? The suits and ties will be in charge.

❑ How about talking the elders of your church into a high-risk investment scheme? High risk of failure.

❑ Want to get your rapping teenager interested in Scandinavian folk music? Ooh-boy, prepare to hit the dirt.

❑ How about convincing your meat-and-potatoes buddy to become a vegetarian? Lots of luck.

It is better to invest your energy in things over which you can have some mastery. This means, sometimes, that your vision for the future has to be adjusted to fit within your realistic sphere of influence. A father is in for trouble if he upsets himself because his son has become a professional skateboarder instead of going to college, studying medicine, and joining the family practice. In our culture and time, we cannot control our children's life choices, and such a situation is tailor-made for depression.

Scaling questions

"On a scale of zero to ten, if zero means you have no control and ten means you have complete control, how much control do you think you have in this situation?" Scaling questions help determine, as accurately as possible, the extent of your power, so you can invest your energies successfully and resign yourself to what you cannot control.

If you find that you are getting more depressed in certain situations or with certain people, perhaps you are trying to control situations that are uncontrollable. Or maybe you're not exercising control in situations where you could have some say. Both extremes are hazardous.

People who believe they have no power over their own lives are the victims. They are primed for depression. Those who believe they have (or should have) complete control are also at risk. Whatever your tendency, you need to recognize your finite freedom and then exercise it appropriately.

Obstacles to Getting Active

My parents used to belong to the American Automobile Association (we called it Triple A). Whenever they went on a road trip, AAA gave them a book of strip maps for their route. Road construction and other obstacles were marked with a rubber stamp, and alternative routes highlighted in yellow. In the days before Interstate Highways, these maps prevented a few wild goose chases. Some of the detours were more scenic than the main road.

As you take the first steps along the path to a better future, you can expect to encounter a few obstacles. It's a good idea to prepare for them in advance.

Unfinished tasks

The feeling of pressure from tasks undone often hinders accomplishment. This pleasure-destroying anxiety is common among depressed students. They have difficulty enjoying a movie or reading a novel because they cannot help thinking about all the homework that has yet to be done in the semester. During the last few days of the term this is appropriate; they ought to be studying. But three weeks into the semester, it is not reasonable to expect all of the term's projects to be completed before one can have a little fun.

If anxiety about things undone (even when they're far in the future) saps your energy for getting things done, you might practice the thought-stopping exercise (see chapter 11).

Or try this: Make a complete list of everything you might possibly have to do in the foreseeable future, leaving room to add more items. Write the dates when you will begin doing them and when you will finish in big, bold numerals. Post the list in plain sight. When the date arrives, do the task and check it off the list. (Just for the fun of it, start the list with a couple of chores you've already accomplished; then enjoy checking them off with a big, red marker.)

Every time you feel anxious about one or more of those looming tasks, take a look at the list. Say out loud, "I'm not supposed to start working at that for another two weeks yet." Then get on with the present.

Procrastination

The same pressure from tasks undone can afflict depressed individuals who procrastinate. Remember the law of inertia? Lacking energy and gumption, the depressed sometimes put off the simplest of chores. As time goes by, these chores magnify until they seem enormous.

For example, six weeks before he is to move, Horace notes that he should send his address change to the post office. Feeling too tired and low to pick up the proper form or take care of it online, he tells himself he will do it tomorrow. Three weeks after the move, tomorrow still waits. Horace's affairs are a mess because of lost and misdirected mail, and the undone task hangs heavily over every chance for enjoyment.

Remembering the positive end of the law of inertia can help those who procrastinate tremendously. Wash one dish. Stir the paint. Pay one bill. Take one tiny bite out of the task you are delaying.

Anxiety

Stress or anxiety can affect both the performance of an action plan and the enjoyment of pleasurable events. Persons who suffer significant stress or anxiety attacks are less likely to enjoy what they do, especially if they are depressed.

If you tend to be an anxious person, just recognizing it will help you work around it. Plan for relaxation breaks when your activities seem too difficult or stressful to carry out. A stress-free detour from your steady progress is not a bad thing. Enjoy the scenery! (See chapter 7 for additional relaxation tips.)

Either/or thinking

It's all or nothing with some folks. They're either fabulous successes or miserable failures. Perhaps they believe they must accomplish every iota of their action plan (and do it perfectly). If they can't, they feel that they've botched it, failed, wasted all their time and effort.

Does this ring a familiar bell? If grandmother called during your exercise time, did you feel terrible for not doing it that day? If at first you don't succeed, do you tend to give up the effort?

You'll feel better about yourself, and make progress in the long run, if you can trim your expectations. This isn't all going to happen according to plan (unless, of course, you've planned for obstacles and detours). Try to view your progress realistically. Be kind to yourself.

External obstacles

Sometimes, what you can accomplish is determined by external factors. For example, let's say you're trying to learn more assertive behavior. You want to stand up for yourself and shed the doormat suit. Unfortunately, you have a boss who really likes to be boss. This could be an obstacle, because you'll either make things harder on yourself at work by standing up to this tyrant, or you'll cave in and feel terrible because you weren't assertive.

But you already know about your employer's authority problem, don't you? Using a little foresight, you can plan a detour—such as, "I'm not going to act assertively with Mr. Perkins because he couldn't handle it, poor thing. First I'll try sticking up for myself with someone safe, like a door-to-door salesperson. Then maybe I'll have a chat with the postal worker who puts my mail in the wrong box."

Keeping up the Momentum

On cross-country car trips, enjoying detours is a strategy for maintaining forward motion in a pleasant manner. No point complaining about the time we've lost; at least we didn't have to turn back. And would you look at that grove of red maple trees! We'd never have found this great antique store if we stayed on the highway. How about stopping for a picnic in the shady meadow up ahead?

Consider some of the following ideas for keeping up your forward momentum as you move into action.

Choose enjoyable actions

When choosing a course of action for conquering your depression, you need to examine whether the actions you've selected are worthwhile and enjoyable to you. For example, if you have experienced a loss of meaningful and pleasurable experiences or relationships, you need activities that can put some of that pleasure and quality back in your life:

- ❏ I will take my border collie to the dog park, where there's a chance to chat with other dog lovers.

- ❏ I will bring a welcome treat to new families in my neighborhood. I don't have to say much when I deliver it—but who knows? I may meet somebody I like.

- ❏ I enjoy reading the Bible; next week I'll try out the Bible study group my neighbor told me about. If I like it, I'll keep on attending.

Remember how much fun Roger had making his flowcharts? He wasn't ready to call it fun, but he liked it enough to make a dozen more. When you enjoy an activity, you are almost guaranteed to succeed at it.

It's not what you do that counts . . . what counts is *doing* it. Move. Act. Do. Almost any action (within legal, ethical, and caloric limitations) is better than doing nothing. Maybe you won't exactly achieve much at first. Don't worry about it. Just moving down the road is achievement enough for now.

Progressing in chunks

My wife and I make a "journey of a thousand miles" at least twice every year, when we drive from Texas to our Minnesota cabin and back again. Actually it's 1,225 miles. The distance could be pretty daunting, but we break it into chunks. While Karen is driving, I fiddle with the radio. When I'm at the wheel, she reads aloud from a good mystery. Every so often, we read the odometer and exclaim, "Look at that! We've gone a tenth [a fourth, a third] of the way!" A certain truck-wrecking yard in Kansas is the halfway point; as we drive past it, we raise a little cheer. These mileposts make the journey seem shorter. Hey, it works. Don't knock it.

You already know to break your task into small, doable chunks. At the beginning, you may even need to break your *day* into short, manageable periods.

It may be helpful to schedule each day's activities on an hour-by-hour basis. When you first get out of bed, the next sixteen hours may seem an eternity, but you can face the next thirty minutes.

If you have been quite depressed, accomplishing a few basic maintenance activities around the house is enough at the beginning. For example: 7:30 A.M.: Strip the sheets off the bed and schedule my day. 8:00: Make coffee. 8:15: Drink coffee. 8:30: Eat a bowl of cereal with yogurt. 9:00: Take the dog for a walk. 9:30: Feed the dog, take a second cup of coffee on the deck. 10:00: Wash the breakfast dishes. 10:30: Put the sheets in the washing machine. And so forth.

If an hour seems like a long time, break it into quarter hours. If scheduling a whole day is too complicated, have a second planning session at lunchtime. Never plan to accomplish more than you know you can do.

Perhaps by now you're convinced that the law of inertia can work for you. The positive half of it (a body in motion tends to remain in motion) is a Powdermilk Biscuit for the melancholic's soul. Do just enough to get moving. Put forth effort, but keep your actions within the range of what's doable. If possible, choose activities you can enjoy.

If you set out to do what you are able to do, success can become a habit. Wouldn't that be "tasty and expeditious"?

TAKE ACTION

A body at rest tends to remain at rest; a body in motion tends to remain in motion.
How can you break out of inertia? What methods will help you to do what needs to be done?

✓ Review events or actions from your past that overcame lethargy.
✓ Write them in a notebook if you like.
✓ Don't say, "I've never managed to overcome lethargy." You've done it (trust me on this), but you may not have recognized it. How did you trick yourself into doing an unpleasant task? When did you do something worthwhile even though you didn't feel like it?
✓ Think of such actions as "inertia busters." Recognizing your past inertia busters can help you get moving forward with comfortable, familiar actions that have already succeeded for you. It can keep you moving forward.
✓ Using one of your inertia busters, take on a small task that needs to be done, one that you can accomplish today (or in the next day or two). Do it.

FOR THE FAMILY

One way to help a family member who is depressed is to spend time doing something together.

✓ Do something fun. Don't necessarily expect the depressed person to enjoy the fun activity, but also don't let that stop you from doing it. No need to go overboard; this can be something very simple like having a meal together, perhaps one in which everyone participates in the preparation, such as top-it-yourself pizzas or fondue.

✓ Marriage or family rituals, such as evening walks, playing games, family devotions, or hugs-all-around, lead to a greater degree of family satisfaction and cohesiveness. Continuing or initiating these rituals when a family member is depressed is important. You need them more than ever.

CHAPTER FOURTEEN

Effective Action: If It Works, Do It!

IN THIS CHAPTER YOU WILL:

✓ Increase and expand your awareness that action is essential to triumphing over depression.
✓ Find out what kinds of activities are more effective than others in combating depression.
✓ Design your own personal action plan to include some of these activities to help you get going and keep on improving.

Everyone I have known to overcome depression, without exception, first got moving. Action is essential to prevailing over melancholia. You need to get active and stay active at tasks that are meaningful, beneficial, and even enjoyable.

Certain kinds of activities are more effective than others in combating depression. Designing your action plan to include some of these jewels will help you get going and keep on going. They will nourish your hunger for purpose and pleasure in life.

Meaning-filled Activities

Perhaps you have read or heard about Victor Frankl's famous little book, *Man's Search for Meaning* (1963). Frankl was imprisoned in a German concentration camp during World War II. There he observed that people who perceived meaning in their painful situation had fewer tendencies to ward depression and more energy to devote to living. Those who did not carve out meaning inevitably died.

Frankl pointed out that meaning does not come to us out of the blue; we must seek it, strive for it, carve it out. It is necessary for survival.

In all circumstances of life (not just in concentration camps), those who connect their lives to something greater than themselves are less likely to suffer depression. This something can be a social cause, a satisfying marriage, or a deep commitment to one's religion and relationship to God.

If you find purpose in your life, and put that purpose into action, you will be better equipped to manage dark times (see chapters 19 and 20).

Interpersonal activities

If you struggle with depression, you need to feel appreciated, accepted, valued, and liked. You need positive involvement with other people (see chapters 16 and 17).

You will be more likely to carry through if you choose activities that have special meaning for you. A depressed amateur radio operator could show his radio gear to interested novices. A lonely single person might join a quilting group, walk in fun runs, or take dog obedience classes (accompanied by Spot)—wherever people are enjoying a mutually good time. An elderly widower might play golf with a few buddies in the summer and shoot pool at the senior citizens' center during the winter. An avid reader might join a book discussion group.

Skill-based activities

You will build self-confidence and gain a sense of achievement if you find activities that show your independence and capability at a task. For example, Jill takes on a special project at work that is beyond the normal requirements of the job and allows a little creativity and independence. Shana volunteers to play the piano for informal Wednesday night worship at her church. Corey agrees to teach computer skills to senior citizens at a community center.

Our old friend Roger might have trouble finding ongoing rewards in pumping gas, but his analysis of this simple activity revealed a sense of order and sequence that he could use in some other technical pursuit, such as restoring antique engines or developing his own photographs.

Pleasurable activities

You deserve to have some delight in your life. Even if you think you have lost the gift for joy, treat yourself with activities that offer intrinsic pleasure (or would, if you were feeling better). You could go out for dinner at a nice restaurant, lie on the beach, attend a favorite sporting event, or take a drive in the country to see the autumn colors.

In short: interpersonal, competence-enhancing, enjoyable, and meaning-filled activities help people who struggle with depression become active participants in life. These are not fillers for idle hours, but core behaviors that can help you break out of the doldrums, catch the wind, and sail in a more purposeful direction.

A Dozen Easy Exercises That Enhance Success

You probably know better than I do that certain actions (or inactions) can make your depression worse. Let's not dwell on those.

Other actions, if practiced faithfully, can ease your distress and raise your spirits. If you feel depressed, you need to make behavioral changes that will improve your frame of mind and manage your depression. The following methods and exercises can help you move into a more active and hopeful mode of existence. Use any of them that address your particular situation or strike your fancy.

Confidence building

We keep coming back to Roger. I like Roger. When his confidence was zilch (a common complaint of those struggling with depression), he wouldn't try anything. In that state, he had a zero to minus ten chance of overcoming his depression. Making all those flowcharts of his abilities began to zap him out of his funk.

But what if he had stopped there? All of his initial, positive effort might have been wasted. Roger needed a more comprehensive program of confidence building to elevate his estimation of himself and his abilities, keep it up, and build upon it.

If you're not terribly depressed but suffer from low self-esteem, a confidence-building program is useful and enriching. If your melancholia is more severe, it could save your life.

Exploration

First, explore past activities that have helped you become more confident, and therefore less depressed. Ask yourself: "What specific things was I doing whenever my depression got even a little better?" Write them down. This inquiry is great because it focuses on your strengths and past successes.

If this sounds a little familiar, you are right: in effect, you are looking for exceptions (as discussed in chapter 11).

What if your first response is that "nothing worked" or "I just came out of it; I didn't do anything to make it better"? What if you gravitate to negative events in your past and avoid looking at positive acts that helped you manage even a tiny aspect of your melancholia? To fight this tendency, you could use thought-stopping (chapter 10). Or you could write all of your reflections in a notebook and then cross-out every negative item on the list.

Venn diagram

Another helpful and interesting tool might be a modification of the Venn diagram (a pictorial device ordinarily used to compare and contrast two of something). Take a pencil and draw two large overlapping circles. The outside of the left circle will represent things you did that made your depression worse. The outside of the right circle will be for things you did when melancholy was absent or when things were better. The elliptical space where the circles overlap is for neutral activities. Before you begin filling up the spaces, make the left side smaller by half (scratch out the part you are leaving out) and enlarge the right circle as much as your paper allows. It doesn't have to look pretty.

When a past action comes into your mind, write it in the appropriate space. What goes where will depend on you. (If you were moderately depressed you probably would write "I tied my own shoes" in the neutral space; but if you couldn't even dress yourself, tying your own shoes would be a very positive activity.)

As soon as the left outside space is filled, stop recording negative behaviors. If you feel compelled to keep on listing them, write on top of the other ones (that's right, they'll be unreadable). Continue listing items in the positive and neutral areas, writing small so there will be room for more as you think of them.

Brainstorm

Next try a little brainstorming. Add to your positive action list a few items you haven't tried but thought might work, especially if they sound attainable and fun.

Once you have researched your past for examples of helpful and healthful behaviors, and added a few fresh suggestions to boot, you are ready to structure a confidence-building program. In other words, you will plan and do actions that have a high chance of success.

❑ List specific steps you will take.

❑ Write them where you will see and use them (not on the back side of an envelope!).

❑ Before you go to bed tonight, choose the first step you will take.

Down the road, you will review your program and evaluate what specific actions seem to be providing the greatest benefits.

Quick action plan

Many weight reduction programs offer their clients a quick weight loss option. It's encouraging to see the pounds drop off in a hurry. (Alas, quick weight loss often ends up causing long-term weight gain because your cells cry out "We're starving here," and your metabolism slows down to store fat for survival.)

Don't worry; a quick action plan for combating depression will not let you down in the long run. It's not an easy fix, but rather a contingency plan that you can put in use at a moment's notice.

A quick action plan can be a lifesaver after depression starts to lift. Once you've gotten accustomed to feeling better, you may not to want to admit that those old feelings are creeping up on you again. When walking in the bush in South Africa with a guide, I saw him take the rifle off his shoulder and hold it in his hands. Knowing that a leopard had been spotted in the area I asked him, "Is this where you saw the leopard yesterday?" He nodded "yes" and kept a watchful eye.

Know in advance what the danger signs will be. Would you go walking in African lion territory without an armed guide? Have your ammunition ready.

This quick action plan works for many people. It has worked for me. I urge you to consider it.

❑ On a small card, write a statement such as: "If I begin to feel low [sad, depressed] in the future, I agree to start doing at least two of the following things today."

❑ In the "If" part of this sentence, you may want to include specific signs of recurring depression, such as not returning phone calls, skipping meals, or sleep disturbance.

❑ Then list specific activities that have helped you with present or past periods of depression.

❑ Also include other actions that you think will be effective in staving off a recurrence.

❑ You might ask a spouse or friend to add suggestions.

The following are sample items that others have listed on their cards:

❑ Go tell a close friend about it.

❑ Continue or increase cardiovascular exercises [running, working out at the gym].

❑ See my doctor [psychiatrist, counselor, minister] immediately.

❑ Go out to lunch with a friend.

❑ Resume taking my antidepressant pills.

❑ Go to the Saturday men's breakfast with the group.

Put the card in your wallet. Carry it on your person at all times. If you begin to perceive even one sign of depression, choose two items from the list and begin to do them *that same day*. The card is a promise to yourself that you will do something positive as soon as you sense melancholy knocking at the door.

> **If you start spiraling back into depression, sometimes it is too late to design and follow a beneficial course of action. With the *quick action plan* you make those vital decisions in advance, while you are fairly strong and clear-headed. *Why not make one now?***

Take on a family member's depression

Family members can provide valuable support for behavioral change. Cloe Madanes (1984, 173) tells of counseling a young woman who could not break out of her depression. Madanes directed the woman's father to take over her depression for a week so his daughter could pursue other interests and get some things done.

Family members who agree to this exercise must act weighted down, sad, and helpless. The depressed get a week's reprieve, and they should accomplish as much as they can during the break. After the week is over, both people return to their usual positions.

This can't possibly work! How can your always cheerful sister-in-law put on a gloomy worldview like a borrowed coat? How can you possibly trade your sadness and low self-esteem for her upbeat attitude?

It shouldn't work, but it does. Often melancholics who have handed over their suffering for a short period of time discover they have more freedom than they had realized. They find that their depression is subject to change and control. They dis-identify from their depression (see chapter 11). You are not your depression and your depression is not who you are, remember?

This swap will let you accomplish more, and your increased accomplishments can lead you to feel better. It also may provide your family member with some insight into the experience of depression to better support you in your progress.

Work outside the home

Having a place to go and something to do in the morning can be uplifting (as long as it's not something you dread). Even after a wonderful vacation, it can be energizing to dress neatly, jump in the car, and head off for work. You feel kind of important.

People who are unemployed, retired, or at home with their children often experience lifted spirits when they find paid or volunteer employment. Work outside the home is not so much a behavioral method or exercise, but a *strategy*. It gets you out of bed in the morning. It provides a structure for your days. It usually places you in an environment where you must interact with other people. It even requires that you carry out certain activities whether you feel like it or not. Work outside of the home, therefore, has considerable potential to lift you out of depression.

What if you have no skills or experience? Volunteer work is a great way to begin. Talk with a volunteer coordinator at the local hospital or any social service agency to find the best use of your abilities. You will be appreciated. Have you volunteered in the past? Put it on your resume. The value of what you do has nothing to do with a paycheck.

Perhaps you think you won't be able to find a position, or you're afraid of getting stuck in a job you don't like. Why not start out with a temporary employment service? Temps are not what they used to be; they handle just about any kind of work under the sun. You can start out sampling a variety of jobs. When you do find something satisfying, you can make it permanent if you like. Think of it as research, an experiment, practice.

Structuring daily tasks

Of course, it's your choice to stay at home. You may have a disability. Perhaps there are young children in your care. Or maybe you just don't think you're ready to face the world. There's a behavioral strategy for you as well. If you want to prevail over your low mood, you will need to structure your days.

Sometimes it helps to sit down at night or first thing in the morning and write a list of tasks that you commit to doing in the day ahead. Include only what you reasonably expect to accomplish in one day. The tasks must be doable and very specific.

Does a whole day seem like too much to structure? Just plan your morning. If it helps, assign specific time frames for each task. At lunchtime you can reevaluate and modify your list. Are you mentally exhausted from a structured morning? Do something relaxing in the afternoon—but write it down in your schedule. Thus it won't be a wasted afternoon, but a planned and needed rest.

If you do not want to take on much at first, begin nominally. On the first day, structure only one task for each period of the day (morning, afternoon, evening)—or even just one activity for the day if that's what you can do. Each day add one very small task that will stretch you a little and offer a greater sense of accomplishment. Be sure not to pass judgment on the value of the things you are doing (as trivial, routine, etc.). Simply do them.

Diversion

Diversion serves those who find that their depression is worse during a certain part of the day (typically the morning) or week (typically weekends). If this is true in your case, this method may be for you.

Beforehand, you can plan diversionary tactics for such times. Take Jerry, a retired man who lived alone. Every morning he felt very depressed and had difficulty facing his work around the house. He missed the cheerful morning sounds his late wife used to make (filling the coffeemaker, banging the mop, even flushing the toilet!). He would putter at one thing or another until his chores stretched into the afternoon.

Jerry's diversionary tactic was to get up at 6:30, his usual time, finish all his household tasks by 8:00, and leave the house until noon. Getting out of the house did not always mean going to another place; sometimes he just tended the garden or sat on the patio and read his hobby magazines. Out there, he didn't hear the silence of his wife's absence. Jerry's morning diversions were a major factor in managing his depression during those difficult early stages.

Teach a friend how to get depressed

I once counseled a successful, thirty-three-year-old bank examiner who seemed to have everything going for him. Bernard had a high-paying job, a supportive wife, and a charming seven-year-old son, yet he was depressed. He had experienced several previous periods of depression that lasted from two to six months. After our opening conversation, I said to Bernard, "It seems to me that you have learned a lot about depression. I would like you to teach me how to get depressed. Help me understand how you do it."

He replied with a rehash of everything he had already told me; he believed that depression just came over him, randomly and uninvited, leaving him powerless to change anything in his work, his home, or his own feelings.

This is a typical first response to the "teach me how to get depressed" challenge. I suggest that you create a scenario with a willing friend. Your friend should drill you on the how-to of becoming depressed:

❏ What things do you do just before you start feeling low?

❏ What's the first thing you do when you get up in the morning?

❏ What do you do right after work?

❏ What do you eat for breakfast/lunch/supper?

❏ Is your evening different in any way?

❏ What time do you go to bed?

❏ What things do you stop doing?

❏ What words do you say to yourself?

❑ How do you work/eat/dress/talk/play differently?

Once you have taught your friend how to get depressed, the next set of questions focuses on those times when your depression recedes:

❑ What things do you do just before these bad feelings start easing off?

❑ What actions seem to reduce the impact of your depressive feelings upon your work or your home life?

❑ How do you finally get to the point where you are tired of sitting around the house and decide to go back to playing golf with your buddies?

The purpose of such questioning, besides helping you become more aware of the specific things that lead you into depression, is to help you recognize that you have some control over your melancholia—or at least over how you respond to it. By consciously choosing certain activities, depressed individuals can lessen the impact of their unhappy condition.

Bernard—as one might expect from an accountant—put together a clear and organized list of things he does before becoming depressed (such as working late but getting less done, watching more television, and avoiding sex), as well as concrete actions that come just before a lifting of his mood (such as timing tasks to finish them quickly, helping his son with school work, and expressing more affection to his wife).

Next Bernard transformed what he had taught me about getting in and out of depression into a specific plan. He conscientiously followed his personal antidepression plan, and has learned to stave off or lessen the effect of melancholy in its initial stages, before its painful effects spread the gloom to those he loves.

Any method that sheds light on your own experience of depression will provide data for a custom-tailored plan of action that suits your own personality and situation. If you follow though, it's bound to succeed.

Writing a positive journal

Writing in a personal journal can furnish you with a powerful tool as you struggle out of your low times. It is important to write only positive things you do or good things that happen. (What if your notes drift off into negativity? *I never do anything right; my life is miserable; I'm sad, so sad.* Tear out the page! Don't just throw it in the wastebasket—it might sit there accusing you until trash pick-up day. Burn it, shred it, get rid of it.)

There are other benefits of a daily journal. Writing (as opposed to thinking) is a physical action. It adds discipline to your life and thus a sense of control. The record of your positive behaviors can help immeasurably in planning new activities.

Take care of yourself

All of yourself. Most people are under one sort of stress or another. It may be pressure at work, a decaying marriage or love relationship, or a houseful of children and chores to manage. Whatever it is, it's tempting to rush around putting out fires and doing what's urgent rather than what's important. When you're under a lot of stress, you may take care of everybody else and neglect to care for yourself.

Depressed or not, if you will do just a few basic self-care tasks without fail, you are certain to see some positive results in your outlook. (Note that some of these tasks were already mentioned in chapters 6 and 7, but in the interest of completeness are listed below with the others.)

❏ *Exercise* (you knew I'd say this, didn't you?) can provide marvelous results in coping with depression. (See chapter 7 for more information about exercise.) Do not, however, ruin your chances of success by training for a marathon. Begin with what you can do quite easily and enjoyably. A half-hour's walk at a comfortable pace, twenty-five minutes on a recumbent bicycle in front of a good TV show, or forty-five minutes of gardening will do you more good in the long run than a five-mile run. Why? Because you are more likely to do it regularly and less likely to injure yourself. Another good reason for exercise: After a half hour or so of vigorous exercise, most people experience the release of endorphins in their body that naturally elevate mood and provide extra energy. The only time not to exercise is the last two hours before bedtime, as the natural energizing effect of exercise may make it more difficult for you to get to sleep.

❏ *Cut out caffeine.* If you really need your morning coffee, switch to decaf. You may have headaches for a few days, but it's worth it; the effect of caffeine (especially when taken with sugar, as in coffee and donuts) can be a downer after the first rush is over.

❏ *Restrict alcohol use.* If you are seriously depressed, you should not drink any alcoholic beverages because alcohol is a natural depressant and will only make you worse. It also may interfere with your sleep, which is bad because sleep disturbance is already a problem for many people struggling with depression.

❏ *Eat nutritious meals.* You don't have to be a health fanatic; just acquaint yourself with basic nutritional needs. Eat lots of fruits and vegetables (disguise them, if you need to). Steer away from fast food, not only because they're full of fat and empty calories, but also because they may contain preservatives and other chemicals that some people experience as affecting their mood negatively.

❑ **Adopt a pet**. If you dislike animals, a pet is not likely to improve your mood. But a dog or cat needs attention and affection, is your friend when you are reticent to be with humans, and expects to play or go for walks with you when you don't feel like it. This is good! Stroking a pet is calming and lowers the heart rate. Taking the responsibility for a furry companion's care is a positive step. You take control in one small part of your life and succeed at something that is important.

❑ **Look your best**. Before you go to bed at night, set out a nice outfit, including underwear and shoes, so you will not be tempted to slip into sweats or stay in your bathrobe. Do this even if you'll be at home alone all day. Trust me on this.

❑ **Bathe** when you need it most. Nervous and sleepless at bedtime? Soak in a warm bath. Dead tired in the morning? Try a tepid shower and move the control gradually to cooler water. Between baths, take a few seconds to splash cold water on your face; you'll be surprised at how good it feels.

❑ **Treat yourself**—not with things that are bad for you, but with beneficial things that you would like. Get a massage. Go to a movie or play, listen to music, feed birds in your backyard, tinker in your workshop, or have a pedicure—whatever *you* would like to do (and not necessarily what others think you ought to do).

You can find meaning and purpose in your existence. Almost any kind of action will improve your well being, but the most hope-producing activities focus on building confidence, expanding relationships with others, and bringing pleasure back into life.

Once you find what works for you and then do it, you regain a greater degree of control over your life. You capture a sense of purpose. You feel better about yourself. In fact, you feel better, period. You're moving into the future.

TAKE ACTION

Take effective action.

This entire chapter has focused on action—activities that can provide meaning and success in your life. *Choose one that seems appropriate to you and start doing it today.* If it is morning, do it before lunch. Put the book down and do it now.

✓ If you are just beginning to climb out of depression, it might be wise to do the Venn diagram (pages 160–61) and immediately follow with Brainstorming (discussed on page 161). Write down your ideas in a small notebook and carry it around with you. When you get another idea, take out your notebook and write it down. Then put your ideas into action.

✓ If you are not depressed now—or not as depressed as you were earlier—then I suggest that you make a Quick Action Plan (pages 161–163). This will prepare you for down times you may experience in the future. The next time you start feeling yourself slipping into depression, you will have a specific plan of action and, perhaps more important, the commitment to combat low feelings with effective action.

✓ Keep moving.

FOR THE FAMILY

Make your own Venn diagram.

I described the Venn diagram above and how it can help a person struggling with depression begin to move out of it. You can modify the Venn diagram for yourself, as a relative or friend of someone struggling with depression. Follow the directions for drawing your diagram:

✓ The outside of the left circle will represent things you have tried to do to help the family or the depressed family member that, if anything, made it worse.

(continued)

- ✓ The outside of the right circle will be for things you have done that seem to help things get better.
- ✓ The space where the circles overlap is for neutral activities, things that didn't seem to help or hurt.
- ✓ When a past action comes into your mind—something you or the family did that *was aimed to help the depressed person,* write it in the appropriate space. What goes where will depend on you.
- ✓ As soon as the left outside space is filled, stop recording negative things. If you feel compelled to keep on listing them, write on top of the other ones (of course they'll be unreadable; that's sort of the point).
- ✓ Continue listing items in the positive and neutral areas, writing small so there will be room for more as you think of them.
- ✓ Carry the Venn diagram with you for a couple of days and add to it as ideas come to you.

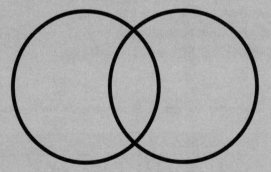

Now Brainstorm:

- ✓ Add to your positive action list a few items you haven't tried but think might work—especially if they sound attainable and enjoyable.
- ✓ Once you have researched your past for examples of helpful and healthful behaviors, and added a few fresh suggestions, you are ready to put your ideas into action.
- ✓ List specific steps you will take. Write them down.
- ✓ Decide what would be an appropriate first step.
- ✓ Now you are planning activities that have a high chance of success.

CHAPTER FIFTEEN

Living with a Depressed Person: The Interpersonal Face of Depression

IN THIS CHAPTER YOU WILL:

✓ Reflect on the fact that depression breeds and propagates.
✓ Learn how it affects spouses, families, and even close friends or coworkers.
✓ Look at studies that have found married people experience *less* depression than those who are single.

My wife and my eldest granddaughter have a little running joke. "If you had a fan club," they tell one another, "I'd be the president." "I'd be the CEO." "Well, I'd be the *emperor* of your fan club." They're joshing, of course—but who wouldn't like to have a fan club?

Who wouldn't like to joke around with someone on such a loving topic?

This lucky woman also works in a school where compliments bounce off the walls. Children are encouraged to compliment their peers. Educators admire each other's work as well as their clothes, their hairdos, their cheerful smiles—whatever is praiseworthy or even just nice. The principal puts notes of appreciation in staff members' boxes.

Who wouldn't like to work in such a nourishing environment?

Depression Affects Relationships

We all need to be loved and appreciated. We need relationships that feed and sustain us. Unfortunately, there's not enough affectionate joking around in relationships with people who are depressed. Soul-nourishing compliments are few and far between. Melancholia breeds and propagates; it tends to affect spouses, families, and even close friends or coworkers. Sometimes the depressed seem to receive no pleasure from the little things others do for them.

Nicole was a secretary to Tess, the owner of a small real estate company. Of late, Nicole had been slow, withdrawn, and weepy. On the way to work one morning, Tess stopped and bought her flowers. Nicole was a good secretary and friend—considerably off her form at the moment, but deserving of appreciation. And she had always loved flowers. "So why," Tess asked her associate late that afternoon, "didn't Nicole seem to notice them on the desk? Why did she just leave them lying there to wilt?"

Depression can throw a wet blanket on once-lively interpersonal relationships and activities. Demetria belonged to a small, fun-loving circle of friends. They met every Friday evening for margaritas, attended plays and baseball games together, did coffee and chitchat several times a month. When Demetria fell into depression, her three pals tried to cheer her up. They called, dropped in, urged her to join in their fun. Like so many friends of depressed people, they cared and wanted to help, but didn't know what they should do. They began calling less often. Then they gave up. The three of them carried on, but it wasn't the same without Demetria.

Depressed people may not always recognize that, as deeply as they are hurting, the people around them also suffer. Take Duncan. He had come to view himself, the world, the future, and his relationships negatively. To compound the problem, his psychic and physical energy was low, so he had less to give. He often would return a cheery hello with silence, refuse invitations, eat alone, and close his office door. He had all but stopped offering helpful comments and compliments to his coworkers and to his family.

Duncan's irritability, neglectfulness, and negativity made him a rather difficult friend and colleague. He was also distant and distracted with his children, and contributed little to his increasingly unsatisfying marriage. He felt his own pain so keenly that he didn't even know how much it was affecting those around him.

Depression Affects Families

Like Duncan, people who are depressed often lack interest in doing things with others. It has a distressing impact on their families.

Flora tells a friend, "Last night I got into my sexiest nightie and pranced around in front of my husband. Two years ago . . . well, you can imagine! Yesterday, all he did was look at me like I had lost my marbles. I felt like a fool."

Ashley has always been her daddy's favorite. "I drew him this picture," she sobs to her mother, "and he didn't even look at it. He doesn't like my drawings anymore."

One study of families with a depressed member discovered that several essential elements of healthy family living were weakened or damaged. These included such things as communication, problem solving, and the ability to emotionally connect to others (Keitner, Miller, Epstein, & Bishop 1986).

If the melancholia has slowly developed over a long period of time, family members are not always aware that one of their own suffers from depression. "Glenda is just not herself." "Doug is under a lot of stress at work." "Menopause is turning Bonnie into a real pill."

Some family members take it personally: "Bea is off in her own world—maybe she has found someone else." "Will is such an unhappy and lonely boy—where have I have failed as a mother?" "Mom doesn't want to play with me—I shouldn't have been bad."

Usually, when people first slide into depression, family members rally around them. They offer help and support.

Here is a typical scenario: Mother suffers from melancholia. Dad tries to serve as a buffer between the children and his wife. He protects her from the children's demands and the expectations of the outside world. At the same time, he shields the children from their mother's black mood. He takes on some of her customary responsibilities. He tries to counter her negative thoughts with positive comments such as, "It's not as bad as all that" or "I'm sure things will work out for the best." He compliments her and brings her flowers.

But parents, children, spouses, and siblings often feel inadequate. Once Dad and kids fail at their initial attempts to help Mother, the family faces a crisis. She is not meeting their needs. Her once supportive ear is no longer listening. Dad is probably exhausted; after a period of time he becomes less attentive and protective. All of them are at risk of slipping into depression themselves.

If Dad or other family members do not recognize Mother's depression for what it is, they may think she no longer cares for them. They will stop accepting her moodiness and start viewing her as an obstacle to the well being of the family. If the depression continues for a long period of time, they will come up with ways to live independently of her. The children may spend more and more time at their friends' homes. Dad may have an affair (some spouses in his position simply leave).

If you are depressed and reading this, the purpose of these words is not to make you feel guilty. The purpose is to let you know what can happen in the family system when depression enters it. You (and your family) can do something about it.

Depression Affects Marriages

Happy and stable marriages have been found to deter depression. This is good news for people who value marriage and family life.

But when depression has become a feature of a couple's married life, good news is hard to come by. Let's say you come home from a hard day at work, wanting to put your cares behind you for a little while. Who would you enjoy spending the evening with: a lethargic, irritable, reclusive mate, or someone who has energy and interest in things, who is upbeat about your relationship? This is not a hard decision. You can see the problem.

Have you read any magazine articles on marriage in the last decade or so? In general, the message is that marriage is bad for women and good for men. However, research on depression reveals a different picture.

A number of studies have found that married people experience *less* depression than those who are single. Spouses who are emotionally close, support each other, and communicate effectively are protected to some degree against melancholia. Marital conflict, however, increases the chances that at least one partner will have symptoms of depression. Many people suffer both depression and marital discord at the same time.

Melancholia's effects are most deeply felt among those closest to the depressed—spouses, parents, children, siblings, and friends. Bonds of affection, law, or birth hold them together. They may share the same home. They want to help, but often don't know how to go about it. If the depression goes on long enough or happens often enough, it's hard to escape the spreading gloom.

If your loved one is depressed, it's important that you learn effective ways of giving aid, but you also need to guard against depression's impact on your own well-being. Protect yourself. Take care of yourself so that this dear, suffering person's low mood will not bring you down. The next chapter is for you. It suggests specifics of what you can do.

If you are depressed, you need to understand the impact of your troubles upon those closest to you. Understand that you are not to blame. Understand that your loved ones care for you, even if they do not always know how to help. Share this book with them. Together you can restore purpose, joy, and laughter to your lives.

TAKE ACTION

Imitate a TV talk show interview.
Surf through the TV channels on any given day and you're likely to find an interview with someone who has gone through a hard time: drug addiction, rape, sexual abuse as a teenager . . . and depression.

✓ Watch how the TV personality asks questions of the guest. The interviewer is prepared, with a note card or teleprompter full of questions.
✓ Now try interviewing someone you know who has come through a period of depression. Like Oprah or Barbara, do your homework; prepare some questions in advance about his or her experiences and *what was helpful*. Don't badger the person, but be curious about what worked—and didn't work—to fend off the depression. Most people are pleased to be asked about themselves and their experiences. They want to share what helped them.

FOR THE FAMILY

Guard your own well being.
✓ Do not allow one person's low emotions to overwhelm the family.
✓ Differentiate between yourself and the negative mood. Stay in the relationship without getting caught up in the other's emotional turmoil.
✓ Strive to be a nonanxious presence in the family. Use some of the methods described in this book to avoid letting emotions overwhelm you.
✓ Remember that you need to think clearly and calmly in order to provide help and support to the depressed family member.

CHAPTER SIXTEEN

A Healing Network:
What Family and Friends Can Do

IN THIS CHAPTER YOU WILL:

✓ Discover things that family and friends can do to help a depressed person.
✓ Look into the subject of divorce or threats of divorce, which happen often in relationships with a depressed spouse.
✓ Accept that the adults close to a person suffering with depression have a responsibility to limit its impact on the family.
✓ Learn how depression can lead to power imbalances in marriages and families.
✓ Recognize that reestablishing above-board positive communication is a major step forward in overcoming melancholy and counteracting the ways in which depression in a family can lead members to pull away from each other.

Are you suffering with a person who is depressed? Is your mother, father, son, or daughter in the clutches of melancholia? Are you concerned about a friend who is debilitated by low mood?

Trying to help a depressed loved one can be frustrating. You do what you can, but many of your efforts seem to fall to the ground, wasted and unappreciated. Eventually you will find it tempting throw up your hands and quit trying. ***Please don't give up! Read on.*** This chapter is full of good news, because you *can* play a vital role in helping your loved one make strides over depression.

Please note that, in this chapter, the term *family member* is interchangeable with *friend* or *loved one.* Don't rule yourself out if you're not a relative of the depressed.

First, you need to think differently about depression. If you view it as pathology, blight, or shame upon the family, you can offer little help. If, however, you recognize that this dark time can serve a purpose for the relationship by signaling issues that need attention, you have taken a hopeful step forward.

Reframing

Your *frame* is your unique viewpoint on experiences and events. Let's revise the paragraph above: *Framing* the loved one's depression as pathology is unhelpful; *reframing* it as a sign of issues that may need attention and can be changed is both helpful and hopeful. The positive frame always assumes that something can be done. It assumes that there are steps that can be taken.

Even if family members only seek accurate information about the experience of depression and nothing more, that knowledge will result in a frame that is more neutral than negative (see Accurate Information, below). It will allow them to address the issue in a more realistic, informed way.

Sometimes, reframing depression as a biological or genetic condition can keep family members from taking it too personally or reacting in either anger or self-blame. They can see it as a medical condition that needs proper care. They can seek to discover the best ways to treat it. Information about the typical progression of a depressive episode is especially helpful. Families need to recognize that depression will abate with time; it is rarely a permanent condition. Understanding the cognitive frame of those who wrestle with melancholia helps family members realize that those terrible negative statements are not the person's true self, but depression speaking.

Strengths

Some depressed people (and sometimes their spouses and families) develop negative viewpoints about their relationships. Under the influence of melancholia, they tend to view the world and other people through a dark and distorting lens.

It is wise to shift the focus to strengths. This may not be easy; you may need to work at it doggedly. Take care not to dwell on the past or concentrate on problems. Change the subject. All people, couples, and families have some things going for them. The relationship has not always been miserable. You have known joy, mutual delight, and happiness. Once families recognize their strengths realistically, they can use them to begin resolving their problems.

Accurate Information

From the outset, family members need accurate knowledge about depression. It's important not to reframe on the basis of wishful thinking ("She just needs a vacation to lift her spirits," "He'll feel better when he gets a new boss"). Wishes may not come true. You need solid facts to reframe your loved one's depression in more hopeful terms.

It's critical to know how depression affects your family member in all four areas of experience—doing, thinking, relating, and living as a biological creature. I can't stress this point too much. Without such understanding, Walter may think he has done something to cause his wife's depression. Jolene may lament her thoughtless words, spoken in a flash of anger, that (she believes) sent her best friend reeling into despair. Billy may fault himself for his mother's frequent tears. (Families must be especially careful that children do not blame themselves for a parent's depression. Young Tad may think that his father doesn't love him anymore because Dad is showing less interest in him than before the depression started.)

If you haven't already done so, read this book in its entirety. It will help dispel some myths about depression. It provides a base of knowledge about its causes and symptoms, as well as practical actions that will help depressed people improve their well-being.

Local resources can fill in some gaps in your knowledge. Interrogate your physician, bring a list of questions to your counselor or psychiatrist, quiz an acquaintance that successfully conquered depression. In many communities, you will find support groups for the depressed and their families (see chapter 22 for a list of possible resources).You also may be able to find useful information on the Internet; see chapter 22 for a list of Websites that provide reliable, accurate data about depression. (As always when using the Web, be wary of unofficial Websites and chat rooms that may pass off rumor, anecdote, and supposition as fact.)

Asking questions and gaining information can help the family view the depression in a less negative light. Maybe your depressed loved one needs to be understood or supported in specific ways, but hasn't the energy or knowledge to tell you about it. What you learn can help sort out your actions and possible mistakes from the problems that the depression itself has produced.

Threats of Divorce

Divorce or threats of divorce happen often in relationships with a depressed spouse. Even if neither spouse mentions the *D* word, it may be hovering unspoken. The depressed may consider divorce because they envision no hope in marriage and see divorce as the only solution. Spouses may contemplate divorce out of frustration; after living with a "down" person for so long, they are starved for emotional sustenance and may be tired of trying.

Such thoughts are common byproducts of depression. They need not lead to divorce, however.

I'm not saying that the marital problems are insignificant. But depression has a tremendous impact on marriages and families, and it's good to keep in mind that things can get better.

If the depressed person is contemplating divorce, it's important for the spouse to determine if it is a serious threat, or if it's just the depression speaking. What if the mention of divorce is more than an idle, passing threat? What if you, the spouse of a depressed person, are seriously considering ending your marriage because living with a person struggling with depression has you at the end of your rope? I strongly urge that you both stay away from attorneys until you have spent a few sessions in marriage counseling (see chapter 21). If your spouse refuses to go to even one counseling session, go alone. You may discover a more hopeful take on your situation, and you also may learn some strategies that will help improve both the depression and the relationship.

Limiting Depression's Effects

A child prone to temper tantrums may have the whole family tiptoeing around to avoid unpleasant meltdowns ("We can't do that; Jacob will pitch a fit!"). The same dynamic occurs in a family with a depressed member. Everything revolves around the depressive's moods. There is no normal family life.

You must do whatever you can to ensure that depression's symptoms do not dominate the family. This does not mean stripping all control away from your despondent loved one; only that you refuse to allow the family's activities and decisions to orbit around the black hole of one person's melancholia. To this end, review the family's everyday functions and determine ways in which they can carry on with as little disruption as possible.

Family meetings are a useful way to bring about a semblance of normal family life. Couples or families meet weekly (more often if needed) to discuss the basic tasks of living and communicate openly about important issues. This is a valuable first step to breaking depression's hold on a system. It would work for roommates or coworkers as well. In these meetings, you can set clear boundaries that will minimize melancholia's influence over your family's well being.

The "Cheer Up" Syndrome

"Cheer up! Look at the bright side! Things will get better, you'll see!" The depressed hear it all the time. Some people even quote scripture, promising (for example) that "all things work together for good for those who love God" (Rom 8:28).

The cheer-up cure has not worked, does not work, and will not work. Stay out of this trap and help ensure that the depressed person's friends and acquaintances do the same.

If Ronnie is determined to wallow in his despair, let him. If Becky wants to be depressed, that's her choice. Remember this basic rule of thumb: *If it doesn't work, don't do more of it.* If a helpful Norwegian tries to give you directions in a lilting tongue you can't understand, will it help if he repeats it three times? Louder? Of course not! He needs to stop talking and draw you a map.

Family members and friends have failed to argue melancholics out of their depression for hundreds, perhaps thousands, of years. If it doesn't, won't, can't work, it is time to do something different (Stone 1994). However, if someone you care for wants to stop being depressed—states it in so many words—then by all means pitch in and do whatever you can to help.

Power Differences

Think of the balance of power in marriage as a seesaw. It may level out or it may move from one end to the other, but if one rider is many times heavier (or lighter) than the other, it won't work at all. Depression shifts the weight and upsets the balance of power in couple relationships.

Many people suffering from depression are running on empty; their psychic and physical energy is very low. When you add to this energy deficit our Western, male-weighted power structure, you can see why it might be especially difficult for a depressed wife to raise issues and negotiate her power in the marriage. She may sit on her feelings and abdicate her rights in the relationship. Her husband, in a well-meaning effort to care for her, may unwittingly take over many of her daily responsibilities, make decisions for her, and thus compound the effect of powerlessness. This also happens in relationships where the wife has the more forceful personality and the melancholic husband has traditionally followed her lead.

The balance of power between husband and wife is a critical issue when one individual is depressed. Why? Because loss of power and control can lead to lower self-esteem, which makes it harder to take action against depression.

If you live with a depressed person, you need to ask yourself if you have (for the kindest possible reasons) taken over power from your mate. If so, how can you restore the balance of power? Doing so can sometimes make things even more difficult in the short run, but in the long run it is essential for addressing this period of melancholy and preventing or softening any future recurrences of depression.

Social Skills

Felicia didn't mean to be rude. She had been depressed for several periods of time over the years and, like so many others in her shoes, needed to learn or relearn a few social skills. She had lost the habit of saying please and thank you. Often she didn't speak when spoken to—wouldn't answer questions, failed to return a pleasant "Good morning." She'd walk through a swinging door and let it close on the person behind her.

The depressed sometimes shun social events and people. They rarely initiate new friendships. It's not that they are socially inept. (Felicia really *didn't* mean to be rude.) They just lack the energy for polite society, and eventually they get out of the habit. They forget how they're expected to act. With the future looking bleak, it seems futile to expend much energy in relationships with others. Such folks benefit from retraining in whatever social skills they lack.

HOLD IT RIGHT THERE! If your depressed family member hasn't asked for assistance in learning these social niceties, don't volunteer it. Your input is likely to be received as criticism or nagging. Whether or not your loved one has asked for help, it might be wiser to enlist the aid of a neutral acquaintance, minister, psychotherapist, or personal coach.

Communication

Sometimes it seems that people struggling with depression have two styles of communication: bad and nonexistent. Marriages in which one spouse is depressed typically suffer from a dearth of communication or constructive problem solving. Occasionally they interrupt this famine with a binge of angry verbal combat, followed by more emotional restraint (Prince & Jacobson 1995). The angry outbursts lead to feelings of hopelessness, especially because the ensuing period of noncommunication offers no chance for resolving their differences.

Since depression in a family can lead members to pull away from each other, re-establishing above-board positive communication is a major step forward. This may not be easy at first: if your spouse is irritable and negative, it kind of takes the fun out of communicating.

Both spouses need to find ways to communicate more effectively. What if the first step is up to you? Remember that this must be a cooperative effort. It's no good announcing tonight that the two of you are going to have family meetings starting next Saturday morning.

At first you might agree to several ten- to fifteen-minute *sharing times* each week. In the first sessions you will only tell one another how your day has gone—no comments or criticisms allowed. Once these short sharing sessions are going fairly smoothly, you can expand the topics of conversation to non-controversial business ("Would you please call Yard Mavens and ask them to mow our lawn more often?" "Does your brother want us to pick him up at the airport?"). Only after you are able to communicate effectively about neutral events in your lives should you address specific problems in the relationship. You have to take it in easy steps.

No matter what kind of structure you give to this venture, the question you need to ask each other is: "How can we *mutually* improve our communication?"

Problem Solving and Change

Improved communication will raise important issues in a troubled marriage and may provide a vehicle for resolution, but good communication is not enough unless it leads to problem solving. In cases of depression, couples need to learn and use more effective problem solving skills.

For starters, work at negotiating small changes in a few problem areas of the relationship. You who are not depressed may believe that you have contributed everything you can to the relationship. You may feel drained, unwilling or unable to give any more. That is why it is essential to start small; both partners need to experience success in their efforts from the beginning.

It is important to not push for major efforts or sweeping changes. Instead, negotiate very small, specific modifications that can be accomplished in a few days, or a week at the very most. The time period needs to be short and the changes small but significant for your relationship. When the first negotiations lead to success, the two of you can toast your accomplishment and go on to address bigger changes and more important issues.

Conversation

Lisa's husband, Frank, has been depressed for nearly a year. She reads everything she can find on the subject—books, magazines, newspaper articles, Internet postings. In doing so, Lisa has picked up quite a vocabulary for analyzing the causes of depression. When Lisa talks to Frank about his troubles, should she get into these explanations? Should she tell him about his "fear of failure," "secondary gains," or "codependence?"

I wouldn't recommend it. People who are trying to manage their depression do not need analysis and explanations. They need to learn skills for handling difficult times in their lives and ways to put those skills into action. Guessing at the why won't help them arrive at the how. (How can I start feeling better as soon as possible? How can I speak more confidently when I'm with others?)

Talk with a purpose

Talking to your loved one about depression is not dinner table conversation. It has a clear purpose: to help both of you reframe events in order to gain a hopeful perspective on the troubling situation. It encourages the sufferer to accept what truly can't be helped and to design ways of changing what needs to be changed.

Portia, a depressed wife in her thirties, narrates her woes to a close family member at length. Perhaps she feels better after these recitations, but what she really needs is to see her physician to determine whether she has medical problems that can be treated with medication. Portia also needs to begin viewing the events of her life in a more positive way. And, whether she feels like it or not, she needs to act differently—purposefully, humanely, and responsibly.

When talking doesn't help

A lot of well-meaning relatives and friends have invested hours upon hours listening to their depressed loved ones. They commiserate with them, run to their beck and call, and help out with their chores—thereby (unwittingly) perpetuating their melancholic passiveness. If conversation helps the two of you feel better for a while but does not lead your spouse/friend to think or act differently, you need a new strategy. Even if you are walking with someone through the valley of intense emotional pain, feeling better is only a side effect of the real goal: to capture a clear vision of the future and step out into it.

Focus

How do you help someone who is bent on venting negative feelings? Jen was one of those depressed persons who talk, talk, talk about their problems. Since as a rule we err by doing more of the same that never worked in the first place, her sister Darcy tried to redirect the focus of all that talk. "Okay," Darcy asked, "but what is *not* depressing in your life?" Darcy didn't let her sister beg off. She probed a little, urged Jen to find even the smallest exceptions to her low mood.

Your goal, as you help another toward a hopeful future, is to avoid focusing on the pit of the depression. Focused questions will pave the way for solutions, built out of existing skills and positive actions that your loved one is already doing well.

Questioning a Family Member Who Is Depressed

I won't put words in your mouth. You will want to formulate questions that cast light on the unique problem. You will seek to zero in on your loved one's particular strengths and resources, target specific symptoms. The questions you ask will help bring together goals and actions to overcome the depression. No matter how much you have to twist and wring a phrase, find a way to state the questions positively. Use the past tense in referring to problems, present or future tense for goals, skills, and solutions. Plan and practice your questions. Assume that change is already underway: "What are you going to wear when you go for your first job interview?"

Problems—try to find out what immediate difficulties are causing problems

Your first questions will probe the nature of the person's troubles. If there appear to be any thoughts of suicide, take appropriate action immediately. Turn (*NOW!*) to the section on suicide referral, chapter 18. If you have any suspicions that your loved one may be suicidal, get help now. This is no time to go it alone. One does not need to be depressed to threaten, attempt, or commit suicide, but many people who are depressed do all three.

If there is any possibility of medical problems, you need to get the person to a physician. (I know, sometimes it's hard to convince a stubborn adult to go to a doctor, but it must be a priority.)

If your family member or friend has been laid off, fired, or passed over for a promotion, the resulting crisis may have precipitated the depression and your conversation can begin there.

Whatever and wherever it is, find the problem.

The faces of depression—identify the signs of your loved one's depression

It will be valuable to know if the characteristics of your loved one's depression are primarily behavioral, physiological, cognitive, or interpersonal. Refer to the four symptom areas discussed in chapter 3, then cooperate with your loved one to identify a cluster of the most problematic symptoms that first need changing.

Strengths—a place to focus your questions

Ask: *What do you do well?* Depressed individuals have many skills, abilities, and resources that they may have temporarily forgotten or undervalued. Encourage your loved one to remember good or successful experiences from the past.

Ask: *How did you function differently in those positive situations?* If necessary, begin by listing routine skills (such as taking a shower or loading the dishwasher), and build on them.

Goals and first steps—ask questions that open up the future

Ask your loved one: *What are your immediate goals?*

Ask yourself: *What practical first steps can I take to help my loved one manage this depression?*

It is important to develop a long-range vision for one's life, but the task can be overwhelming. At the start, you need to help your depressed family member come up with some realistic objectives or *first steps* that will get the ball rolling and stop the slide into deeper depression (see chapters 13 and 14 on problem-solving).

Noticing Subtle Clues

Some mildly depressed persons only need to tell their story and set goals, and do not want or need any further assistance. For those whose symptoms are not severe and who are highly motivated to get beyond their depression, the supportive care of family and friends is sufficient to help them weather their melancholy.

Note, however, that some people never say to family and friends, "I feel depressed." They may go to their doctor complaining of back problems or sleeplessness rather than despair. They may go to a marriage counselor complaining, "My partner is insensitive to my needs," rather than speaking of their melancholy. They may bring their guilt or spiritual struggles to a minister and not recognize those struggles as depression.

If you have read this far, you already know (or suspect) that your friend or spouse or parent or sibling or child is depressed. You already have detected melancholia lurking behind the insomnia, troubled relationships, or spiritual issues. If your loved one has experienced depression in the past, you recognize the signs of its return.

Perhaps your loved one did not ask for help at all; many who are depressed do not. But you (and probably other friends and family members) have noticed this person's trouble. You care. You're ready to get involved—not with a passive listening ear, but with constructive conversation and pointed questions that move toward solutions. More about helping a depressed person will follow in the next chapter.

Family members endure pain along with their depressed loved one. But through improved communication and effective problem solving, with the benefit of your reframed understanding of this disease, and by taking advantage of professional help and guidance if it is needed, this dear person and all members of your family system can recover. You can face a more hopeful future together.

TAKE ACTION

Share with a friend.
Many people who experience the symptoms of depression keep it a secret. They do their best to keep up a good front. But it is helpful to share your low feelings with a close friend, or with anyone you can trust.

✓ Go to the phone now. Call that person for a lunch date, or stop by your friend's house today.
✓ Don't overburden your friend, but talk honestly about what you feel and what you are doing to address the depression. Who knows—your friend may have been through similar experiences. You won't know unless you try.

FOR THE FAMILY

This entire chapter was written for you.
✓ Read it, several times if necessarily.
✓ Follow the suggestions.
✓ Make sure that depression's symptoms do not dominate the family.
✓ Schedule your first couple or family meeting today.
✓ Start small; remember not to push for major efforts or sweeping changes.
✓ Any change you initiate should be doable in a very short period of time.
✓ When your first negotiations lead to success, applaud yourself for your accomplishment.
✓ Later, if you wish, you can go on to bigger changes and more important issues for the family relationship.

CHAPTER SEVENTEEN

Help for the Whole Family

IN THIS CHAPTER YOU WILL:

✓ Examine research showing that couple and family counseling benefits both the depressed individual *and* the family.
✓ Understand that family therapy is crucial—one might even say imperative—when children and adolescents suffer from depression.

Randall had always been somewhat quiet and shy. From middle school on, he lived and breathed computers. He hung out with members of the computer club in high school. After school they emailed each other, exchanging information about cool Websites. They were nerds—but they were nerds of the future. They *ruled*.

Randall was proud of his DSL connection. He was one of the first in their small town to have it. He spent hours in his room surfing the Web, visiting chat rooms, and researching school papers.

Now something was wrong. Randall's computer was gathering dust. He still sat in his room but no longer chatted with his buddies online. After a while, the computer nerds from school stopped calling. His grades dropped.

Luke and Annette were worried—Annette, especially. Was their son sick? He didn't seem to be. Was he on drugs? They had never seen the slightest evidence of that. Was he just being a moody sixteen-year-old? Luke leaned to that view. They knew from their two older children that teenagers can be cheerful one day and irritable the next.

Was Randall depressed? Luke and Annette argued about it. Annette wanted to see a counselor, but Luke refused: "It's a phase he's going through." Meanwhile, Randall's gloom cast a shadow over the household.

You may know all too well that one person's melancholia is not the only problem in the family or social system. Perhaps the marriage is in serious trouble, whether that trouble is expressed in heated arguments, physical battles, cold silent anger, or just a flat deadness. The family as a whole may be chaotic, embattled, dysfunctional, or disconnected.

When the depression of one individual is accompanied by serious family distress, self-help may not be enough to bring about healing. The following paragraphs will offer a few helpful suggestions for families seeking to uplift not only the depressed loved one, but their family relationships as well.

Couple and Family Counseling

Years ago, Stella's husband, Jack, urged her to get psychotherapy for her depression. She never stopped going. Week after week she shared her feelings with the therapist. She did feel a little better by the end of each session. When she got home, not much changed. The marriage became increasingly unsatisfying for both of them. Of course Jack noticed this, but they kept on paying the therapist's bills. It seemed like the *least they could do.*

Sometimes, couple or family counseling is the *best thing a family can do.* Like Jack, many people urge their depressed loved one to go into therapy—but the trouble is, everybody in the family is suffering. Couple or family counseling can help nondepressed members of the family as much as the depressed person; they learn about the disorder and what they can do to help, thus enabling them to help restore the family to wholeness.

Even though it is unclear whether depression causes or is caused by problems in relationships, research data shows a benefit to couple and family counseling when one member is depressed. A number of studies comparing psychotherapy with and without the involvement of a spouse found that the reduction in depressive symptoms was equal; however, therapy with the spouse's participation was more successful in improving overall marital and family satisfaction (U.S. Vol. II 1993, 79).

People used to believe that you had to treat the depression first, before tackling issues in the marriage. Turns out they were wrong. Whenever there is a depressed person and a troubled relationship, marriage and family counseling is a preferred model for responding to the depression. It is very effective at improving the relationship *and* the melancholia at the same time. In fact, counseling the troubled marriage or family is tantamount to caring for the depression. Chapter 21 offers specific tips for getting the kind of treatment that will bring about positive results.

Of course, marriage and family counseling is not the only way to care for depression. I have made the point elsewhere in this book that your family needs a multifaceted approach. However, since depression can be a recurring disorder, treating your spouse's present depressive episode with you (and perhaps your children) present not only deals with the immediate distress; it helps protect and prepare your loved ones for the possibility of future episodes.

Helping Depressed Children and Adolescents

At no time is family therapy more appropriate than when children and adolescents suffer from depression. As in adult melancholia, depression in children has physiological, cognitive, behavioral, and interpersonal aspects. However, because children are dependent upon adults, the interpersonal face of their struggles is especially noticeable. When a child is depressed, families suffer. The parents' relationship is stretched thin, and may even end in divorce.

Children are not very good candidates for self-help. They're unlikely to be reading this book. It is up to parents, guardians, grandparents, teachers, ministers, therapists, and other supportive adults in their lives to guide them toward the hopeful future that they deserve.

It is not hard to imagine the impact of a parent's depression on the kids. Depressed parents may not respond to their children as much as they usually would. They are less likely to resolve parent-child conflicts. Their children are more likely to develop depression—especially if there is no attempt at intervention in the family. In some cases, treating a parent's depression helps resolve a child's melancholia.

Several researchers estimate that up to 10 percent of children and adolescents experience at least one depressive episode (Kazdin 1989). It is difficult to pin down the incidence of depression among children and adolescents because they do not always exhibit the blue mood so common in adult depression, and therefore do not report it to helpers. In fact, a *lack* of mood swings or moodiness in adolescents may indicate depression.

Children and adolescents often display their depression by acting out. Some (like Randall) quietly withdraw from people and events. They become moody and irritable. Their grades may go down, and they may have difficulty generating energy for school or extracurricular activities. Children's depression also manifests itself in discipline problems at school, truancy, scrapes with the law, physical illness, and suicide attempts.

Determining whether a child under age twelve is depressed or just painfully shy can be tricky (unless the child was formerly very outgoing). Self-help is not a possibility for these kids; what's called for is consultation or referral to a psychotherapist who specializes in family counseling and child psychology.

Teenagers are more apt to show typical adult symptoms. They may experience sad moods, sleep disturbance, lack of interest in eating or eating disorders, and hopelessness.

Even for those who are not depressed, adolescence is a moody and vulnerable time of life. One day the adolescent may be up and excited; the next day down, grudging, and negative. How do you differentiate between natural moodiness and actual depression? And what about drug use? Some illicit drugs produce symptoms similar to depression.

Adolescence is a time of breaking away from the family and gaining greater independence. When teenagers suffer depression, parents may want to protect them as they would a sick toddler. But even melancholic adolescents want to express their freedom and individuality, and their parents need to allow it.

Parents, though, must still be parents. They can negotiate with their children, searching for the right balance between necessary boundaries and realistic freedoms. They need to keep in mind the realities of this family's unique situation as well as the extent of the child's depression.

Responsible adults need to take action (such as hospitalization or the prevention of suicide) if the depression becomes severe. In such cases it's essential to consult with mental health professionals (again, see chapter 21).

If you care for a child or adolescent who seems to be depressed, do not blame yourself for the young person's troubles. "I've failed my child" is not a helpful lament—and very likely it's not true. As in cases of adult depression, the important thing is to focus on what can be done.

If you have made parenting mistakes, join the crowd. Put them behind you. Capture the good. Follow the suggestions in this book, adapting them as necessary to the age of your child. Do not hesitate to get outside help. Lend a hand as your precious one takes small, positive steps into the future, rejoicing and building on each success along the way.

Melancholia rarely attacks one person at a time. It can spread its distress to life partners, parents, children, and all those near and dear to the suffering one. It is important to recognize that people do not live in isolation. They live in systems of families and friendships. When one suffers, everyone in the system suffers to some degree. When members of the system get counseling together, when they pitch in to help the depressed loved one using knowledge, skills, and effective methods, they also help the entire system regain wholeness and health.

TAKE ACTION

If your relationship with your partner is rocky, it may be time for a tune-up.

✓ Check with a local pastor, rabbi, imam, or priest about marriage enrichment weekend retreats or groups.

✓ Look in the phonebook or check with your local mental health association for marriage enrichment groups.

✓ Check the Website http://members.aol.com/wwmeroch/sectionii.html for a group near you. The following two Websites also can suggest resources: www.bettermarriages.org or www.marriageenrichment.org.

✓ If you suspect that your problems are more severe, see a minister or marriage counselor (see chapter 22).

FOR THE FAMILY

Marriage enrichment or marriage and family counseling can be useful when the effects of depression have spread to the family.

✓ Addressing the marriage relationship in a weekend retreat may also have a positive effect on the symptoms of depression.

✓ If you are concerned that a child or adolescent in the family is depressed, a visit with the family physician is in order. In addition, family counseling for all members of the family can be very beneficial.

✓ When members of the family system get counseling together, they also help the entire system regain wholeness and health.

Part Three

Help for Depression

CHAPTER EIGHTEEN

How to Save a Life: Suicide Prevention

IN THIS CHAPTER YOU WILL:

✓ Examine a list of some untrue myths about suicide.
✓ Consider the signs of suicide and possible interventions.
✓ Follow an important discussion of factors that can indicate serious suicide risk. (This is not meant as a checklist, but rather a guide to listening and watching for telltale signs of lethal peril.)
✓ Remember to take *all* ideas of suicide seriously—the basic rule when dealing with even the hint of suicidal thinking.
✓ Recognize that because the incidence of suicide among depressives is high, assessing risk is only part of the task. The family must *act*.

Amanda was concerned about Sean, her younger brother. His marriage had failed, his job was in jeopardy, and he was clearly feeling depressed. Sean lived alone. For a month, Amanda had been calling him every night to check on him and listen to him for a while. But in the past week, Sean had seemed evasive. He deflected her questions with a terse, "I'm fine." Amanda told her husband that she didn't believe her brother was fine. Could he be planning to kill himself?

Don't wait!	**Do you worry that your loved one may be suicidal?** *If so, it's time for action.* **Without delay, contact a crisis hotline or suicide prevention center. Alternatively, call a physician or other health professional. Do not let the fear of embarrassment keep you from taking necessary action—if you think it's called for—to prevent this permanent and tragic solution to a temporary and treatable situation.**

Suicide, even talk about it, is dramatic and provocative. In fact, I'd rather not write this chapter, because I don't want to scare you. The best way to face the fear associated with suicide, however, is to learn about it. Separate the fact from fiction.

In the box below, I have listed some untrue myths about suicide. After examining these common misconceptions, we will consider the signs of suicide and possible interventions, and list some resources that can help you deal with this crisis.

Never underestimate a depressed person's desire to escape the pain. The agony of severe melancholy is so strong that many sufferers—especially those who are moderately or severely depressed—consider suicide as the only way to find relief. *Three-fourths of all depressed individuals consider taking their own lives.* More than 60 percent of people who kill themselves suffer from depression (U.S Vol. I 1993, 9). If you or someone you know is depressed, you must determine if there is a suicide risk. If any danger signs appear, immediate and appropriate action is imperative. Always remember that despair and loss of hope can have fatal consequences.

Now you know why I have to write this chapter.

COMMON MYTHS ABOUT SUICIDE

It is not necessarily true that . . .

✓ If someone wants to commit suicide, there is nothing you can do about it.
✓ People commit suicide without giving any warning.
✓ It's best not to talk about suicide with depressed people because you may give them the idea to do it.
✓ People who talk about suicide never do it. They may be just seeking attention.
✓ The elderly never commit suicide.
✓ Young people never commit suicide.
✓ Only the severely mentally ill actually commit suicide.
✓ People who commit suicide don't want help.
✓ A person who is suicidal will be suicidal for the rest of their life.
✓ Every suicide is preventable.

Assessing the Danger

The following factors can be indicators of serious suicide risk (Farberow, Heilig, & Litman 1968; Stone 1993). They are not exhaustive. ***They're not meant to be used as a checklist, but as a guide to listening and watching for telltale signs of lethal peril.***

Age and sex

Is the person who is threatening suicide a woman or a man? Old, young, middle-aged? More women than men attempt suicide, but more than half of completed suicides are men. The threat becomes more serious with age, especially among men. A man in his late sixties is four or five times more likely to commit suicide than is a sixteen-year-old girl. However, *you must take all hints or talk of suicide very seriously*. People are not statistics.

Crisis

Has the person recently experienced divorce, the death of a child or spouse, job loss, or a debilitating illness? Crises triggered by loss or impending loss often bring about serious threats of suicide. If the pain is extreme and the person has a specific suicide plan, family or friends need to intervene actively.

Meaning and religion

Strong religious beliefs and regular involvement with a religious group provide emotional support, but they also serve as social constraint against suicide. People who are not connected to any spiritual group or belief system and who do not have a sense of purpose in life have fewer inhibitions about committing suicide. Again, this is only a statistic; sometimes even deeply devout people take their own lives.

Specific conditions

The family needs to be aware of complicating factors such as recent death or divorce, job loss, psychosis, alcoholism or substance abuse, imminent arrest or exposure for a crime or scandal, unusual socially unacceptable sexual activity, and a history of suicide in the family (parent, sibling, child, spouse, or best friend). All of these conditions can significantly increase the risk of suicide.

Resources

Even surrounded by family and friends, your loved one may feel alone, may think that nobody cares. You need to identify others who can help during the crisis—friends, relatives, church members, coworkers, and such. If someone you care about appears suicidal and immobilized, inform two or three of those resource persons about the suicide potential so they can actively communicate their caring to your loved one.

Lifestyle

People who have relatively stable lifestyles—indicated by such things as consistent work history, long marriage and family relationships, and absence of past suicide activity—have a measure of protection against suicide.

Indicators of instability include such things as addiction, hopping from job to job (or from marriage to marriage, lover to lover, apartment to apartment, etc.), mental illness, and frequent unresolved crises. Chronic (repeated, ongoing) suicide threats happen only among people with unstable personalities. Acute (severe, one-time) suicidal gestures occur among the stable and unstable alike. Both are potentially lethal.

Suicide talk

Many people who are depressed talk of suicide, but not always in so many words. Sometimes their comments go unnoticed until it is too late. The family must listen for statements such as, "I'm tired of trying," "Life isn't worth living anymore," "There is no way out," "You and the kids would be better off if I were gone," or even "I've been thinking I should give you these phone numbers to call in case anything happens to me."

Suicidal behavior

People who are contemplating suicide not only express it verbally, they also act it out. They may get their affairs in order, wonder out loud what it's like to die in different ways, make a new will, give away their favorite things, purchase a gun, talk with the family about how to dispose of personal property, and so forth. Look for subtle, nonverbal signs that the person is entertaining thoughts of suicide. They are just as important as direct verbal threats. Any of these gestures must be taken seriously, especially if they are new behaviors.

Suicide plan

You may not know if your loved one has made a suicide plan. (See the "Talk about it" section below.) Any indication that such a plan exists—especially if it is detailed with specific actions and involves a highly lethal method, such as gunshot or jumping from a high place—is by far the most dangerous sign of an impending suicide.

You may happen upon some written notes. The person may speak as if the plan is hypothetical ("If I were going to kill myself, I'd . . . "). Other hints that a suicide plan is forming (or finalized) may be making a will, giving away cherished possessions, or abruptly changing one's normal routine.

Communication

Has the person stopped communicating with others? This may signal hopelessness and a more serious danger of suicide. I know of a woman whose ex-husband was physically disabled, angry, and deeply depressed. When his mood suddenly lifted, she judged it would be safe to go to his house and do a few chores for him. Tragically, he only *seemed* calmer because he had resolved to end his life, and when she arrived, he killed her as well as himself.

If someone you are concerned about no longer talks about their distress and has stopped telling you of their problems, it is not necessarily a sign that he or she is getting better. It may mean that she or he has made the fatal decision and is only waiting for the right time. Get help.

Health issues

The dying or seriously ill may be attracted to suicide as a way of escaping pain and suffering. The family should determine if a possibly suicidal individual has (or fears) a serious disease such as cancer, an impending or recent surgery, or chronic illness.

All of the above indicators need to be taken seriously, but—*except for a detailed and lethal plan*—none is necessarily dangerous by itself. It is important to gather as much information as possible; seek advice from a counselor, physician, minister, or crisis telephone line; and evaluate the whole picture to see if a lethal pattern is forming.

The Family Must Act

Assessing risk is only part of the task. The family must act. The incidence of suicide among depressives is high. Always consider that the depressed person may be contemplating suicide.

What if the person has no family or close friends? What if you are just a concerned neighbor or coworker? Please act *as if* you are a member of the family. You can help save a life.

Take all ideas about suicide seriously

This is the basic rule when dealing with even the hint of suicidal thinking. When a depressed person says, "I'm tired of trying" or the like, family members may think, "Oh, it's just his negative thinking," "She's just trying to get attention," or "It's just talk." Of course, it might be just talk—but how can you know that? Ignoring the signs, even if they seem passing or insignificant, can be a tragic error.

Talk about it

Ask: "Are you thinking about killing yourself?"

Don't wait for your loved one to bring it up, and don't beat around the bush. It simply is not true that discussing suicide will encourage a person to do it; talking about it in frank and specific detail is far, far better than ignoring it. It allows the family to decide how they will respond.

It is good to determine whether suicide is only an indefinite threat, or a specific resolution accompanied by a plan for how to go about it. Have in mind the following questions:

- ❑ How specific is the plan?

- ❑ How lethal is the method?

- ❑ How ready are means for carrying out the plan?

Obviously, a gun is more lethal than some pills. A full bottle of barbiturates is quicker and more certain than a handful of aspirin. It is also good to find out if your loved one has been researching methods of suicide on the Internet.

Act now if the person has spent time thinking in detail about how to commit the act, has formulated a plan and chosen a lethal method, and has access to the means. The risk of suicide can be very great indeed.

When people are contemplating suicide, their family and friends often ignore or dismiss their suicide talk, perhaps because it is too painful to consider. But the depressed need someone to talk to about their suicidal thoughts.

Are you uncomfortable with the idea of suicide? Do you cringe from talking about it? Then refer your loved one to a physician, counselor, pastor, or even another friend or family member who is able to have these tough conversations. If there is the slightest doubt about the risk, refer to a qualified professional. (Call a crisis or suicide prevention hotline, for example. When in doubt, call 911.)

Preventive steps

If a serious risk of suicide exists, the family needs to dispose of all weapons and dangerous drugs. This includes sharp kitchen knives and razor blades, prescription medications, and over-the-counter drugs such as NyQuil. Get them out of the house. If it's necessary medicine, keep it on your person at all times or under lock and key.

When people are seriously suicidal they should not be left alone, not even for a few minutes. A family member or friend needs to be with the person twenty-four hours a day during the acute suicide crisis, which usually lasts only a matter of hours or a few days. If it is impossible for someone to be there at all times and you are gravely concerned, contact the police or a local hospital with psychiatric facilities.

Suicide calls at night

It's 3:00 A.M. and the telephone rings. Your seventy-year-old widowed father is on the line, distraught. It sounds as if he's been drinking. He says, "I can't go on any longer." You've heard this talk before, but something about his mood and the late hour alarms you.

You are right to be alarmed. People can feel more desperate, fearful, and hopeless at night when others are asleep. Family members need to plan ahead for the possibility of nighttime suicide calls. For example: Keep the person on the phone. If you have a cell phone as well as a land line, use the other phone to call for help—call 911 if you think he or she has already taken pills, has a gun in hand, or the like. If you do not live in the same neighborhood, have on hand the phone numbers of the person's neighbors, and don't hesitate to call at any hour when a life is at stake. If necessary, send your housemate out to make the call.

Don't give in to embarrassment. If your car were hanging on the edge of a cliff, would you refuse help because you are ashamed of your careless driving?

Get help now!

If there appears to be a real chance that a depressed person will attempt suicide, you must intervene even more actively. Here are some options:

❑ Contact the person's psychiatrist or counselor.

❑ Take the person to a walk-in psychiatric crisis center, which can be found in many larger hospitals.

❑ Call the police. Family or friends should not be afraid or ashamed to do so; this is the police's job. Sometimes it is the only way to ensure the safety of a person who has temporarily given up on life.

❑ If the person has already inflicted injury or ingested pills, call 911 immediately. Do the same if there is any possibility of physical violence, drug use, alcohol use, or the presence of a gun. It is not unusual for suicidal depressed persons to refuse help from anyone—family, friends, counselor, or pastor—and the emergency crisis team or police need to take over.

In the end, the family must do anything and everything possible to restrain a depressed person from committing suicide. Do the best you can so that if the worst does occur, you can know that you did all that was possible.

When I worked at a Suicide Prevention Center early in my career, I learned that many who were prevented from suicide said afterward they were glad to have been rescued. You may have heard the phrase: *suicide is a permanent solution to a temporary problem*. It's true. No matter how bad the problem may be, there is a way to cope with it tomorrow.

TAKE ACTION

If your depression is bad and you have felt suicidal, it is good to work out a "suicide contract" with someone else—a family member or close friend. You can also do it with a helping professional, such as a clergy person, psychotherapist, or support group leader. In the contract you promise to contact that person (or the local crisis line if the person is not available) if you start having ideas of suicide. You promise to take no action to harm yourself until you have at least discussed it with someone else. Hopefully you never need to exercise your contract, but it is better to have one than not.

FOR THE FAMILY

The responsibility for suicide prevention falls upon family members and friends.
- ✓ This entire chapter is written for the family. Go back and read it carefully. Then read it again. Take it seriously.
- ✓ Make a list of resources you will call in an emergency. Put a copy by each telephone and in your wallet.
- ✓ Never let fear of embarrassment keep you from taking drastic action, if you suspect it's called for, to prevent this permanent and tragic solution to a temporary and treatable condition.

CHAPTER NINETEEN

Desolations: Depression and Spirituality

IN THIS CHAPTER YOU WILL:

✓ Compare depression with the spiritual struggles that people encounter on life's journey.
✓ Discover that spiritual struggles are not relics of a time long past, nor are they the exclusive territory of mystics and members of religious orders.
✓ Find that, in fact, spiritual struggles resemble what psychology calls major depression.
✓ Learn about several spiritual struggles from the history of the church that resemble depression, such as "the dark night of the soul" and others.

How long, O Lord? Will you forget me forever?
How long will you hide your face from me?
How long must I bear pain in my soul,
and have sorrow in my heart all day long? (Psalm 13:1-2)

Imagine the psalmist of the Hebrew Scriptures sitting in a quiet, private space, penning these words. Do they strike a familiar chord? Does his lament sound like something you have experienced? Could it be that the psalmist was in the grips of melancholia? Suffering is a persistent theme in Scripture. See what Job—perhaps the definitive symbol of suffering in all human literature—has to say:

Why did I not die at birth, come forth from the womb and expire?
For my sighing comes like my bread, and my groanings are poured out like water.
Truly the thing that I fear comes upon me, and what I dread befalls me.
I am not at ease, nor am I quiet; I have no rest; but trouble comes.
(Job 3:11, 25-26)

We have seen how depression disturbs important relationships. For the religious, depression disrupts their relationship with God (by whatever name they call their deity). When people feel the absence of God, when they doubt, when religious ritual and service lose meaning, their experiences are very similar to the symptoms of depression.

I think of Craig, the owner of a small printing business. Until one January in his thirty-sixth year, Craig told me, "I loved my work, I loved my wife and kids, and I loved my Lord. Now I don't want to go to work in the morning. I don't want to go home at night, and I don't want to go to church." He used to pray every morning and every evening. Now he rarely prayed.

Craig knew something was wrong. He knew things wouldn't always go smoothly at work or at home, but he never expected this distance from God, this cold dryness of spirit. "God is nowhere to be found," he told me.

Reflecting on the experience of melancholy and spiritual desolation can bring depth and meaning to people of faith. Throughout the ages, devout people have written of despair and malaise. We can learn, from their writings and their experiences, the spiritual impact of depression. We can learn ways that others have found to overcome it.

The historical examples that follow come from the Christian tradition. Similar stories occur in most religions; I lack the knowledge to write about those and will stay in familiar territory. If your background is not Christianity, I urge you to examine your own tradition for comparisons to depression. Look for wisdom within your religion that speaks to your melancholy.

The Noonday Demon

In central Turkey there is a moonscape of a place called Cappadocia. Bizarre formations of volcanic tufa rise from the dry hills. Dwellings, churches, monasteries, and even inns were once carved out of the tufa rock—many of them still in use today. In this weird landscape, perhaps in one of its rock-carved rooms, St. Evagrius of Pontius began his life in A.D. 345.

Evagrius (also known as Evagrian) was a brilliantly gifted thinker at a time when gifted men rose to wealth and power in the church. As a youth he came under the wing of St. Gregory the Theologian, who brought Evagrius to Constantinople (now Istanbul). The imperial city must have dazzled this young man from the country. There, Evagrius rose to a position of considerable influence as aide and advisor to the bishop.

In Constantinople, Evagrius grew proud and arrogant. He became involved with the wife of an official and was forced to flee her husband's wrath. He escaped to Jerusalem, where he was received warmly but in due course got himself into trouble again.

Obviously, Evagrius, was a man of considerable appetites. He also was a man of extremes. His appetites had brought him twice to the point of emotional and physical breakdown; he devoted the remainder of his life to self-denial.

During his last fifteen years, Evagrius lived with a colony of monks in huts on the Egyptian desert some fifty miles from Alexandria. The minimal desert life must have been a stark contrast to the bustle and sensory stimulation of Constantinople and Jerusalem. Evagrius saw many desert monks fall victim to a condition that bears remarkable similarities to depression. He described it as the *noonday demon*:

> The noonday demon makes the sun appear sluggish and immobile, as if the day had fifty hours. Then he causes the monk continually to look at the windows and forces him to step out of his cell and to gaze at the sun to see how far it still is from the ninth hour, and to look around, here and there, whether any of his brethren is near. Moreover, the demon sends him hatred against the place, against life itself, and against the work of his hands, and makes him think he has lost the love among his brethren and that there is none to comfort him. (Wenzel 1967,5)

Accidie

The early desert monks called this noonday demon *accidie* (also known as *acedia*, *accidia*, or *akedia*). Difficult to translate, accidie is a spiritual malaise, lethargy, a dryness—what Evagrius expressed as a struggle with temptations, boredom, weariness, and difficulty maintaining attention or focus. In Evagrius' description, we see all of the faces of depression: the monk experiences physiological slowdown and exhaustion, distorted thinking, immobilized behavior, and disruption in his relationships with God and the other monks.

Perhaps the Psalmist also knew this dryness:

> God, you are my God, I am seeking You, my soul is thirsting for You, my flesh is longing for You, a land parched, weary and waterless. (Psalms 63:1, NJB)

Accedie was, and still could be, considered a form of melancholia that profoundly affects one's relationship to God. It certainly is similar. Can you recognize accidie in Craig's cold dryness of spirit? Do you recognize it in your own experience?

There's no conclusive evidence that Evagrius himself suffered from the noonday demon. However, in his capacity as spiritual advisor, he cared for young monks who were grappling with this lethargy and malaise. He counseled them to "keep careful watch" of its effects on their thoughts and feelings.

Dryness of the Soul

How can one overcome this deadly dryness of soul? Evagrius recommended a life of discipline and self-examination. He gave service to others, thereby very likely guarding against spiritual malaise in his own heart.

Cassian, a sixteenth-century mystic and follower of Evagrius, stated that accidie causes "such fatigue and such hunger that one feels tired as if one has traveled a long way or completed a very difficult job, or as if one were exhausted by a complete fast of two or three days!" (Bringle 1990, 57). He suggested manual labor, tenacity, and endurance as remedies.

Gregory the Great urged "spiritual joy." According to Gregory, "the best cure for despair is an awareness of the possibilities of grace, a cultivated confidence in God's benevolence and ultimate benediction" (Ibid., 60).

In the midst of his depression Craig found it impossible to feel spiritual joy. But he found encouragement in knowing that his noonday demon was an experience familiar to many devout people. Craig needed Cassian's prescription: tenacity and endurance. He returned to his regular prayer and devotional times. He accepted that it really is okay to "go through the motions," that God continues to work in him even when he can't feel it.

Accidie is not a new experience, nor is it a relic of ancient times. People of faith have continued to encounter this spiritual dryness through the centuries, naming it differently and casting new light upon it.

Dark Night of the Soul

Many historical writings on spirituality have made reference to darkness. St. John of the Cross wrote of spiritual desolation in his book, *The Dark Night of the Soul*. You feel vulnerable and recognize your finitude. You yearn for connection with the Other, but perceive little or no response.

For the Christian, the dark night of the soul is not synonymous with depression. It is part of the journey of faith. This image of a journey has long served as a metaphor for religious experience. Throughout the ages, billions of people have undertaken pilgrimages—to Jerusalem, Assisi, Mecca, the Ganges River, the Catacombs, Nuestra Señora de Guadalupe, Mount Fuji, the Great Mosque of Damascus, Mt. Ararat, Canterbury, Bethlehem, Lourdes, and literally thousands of other sites—out of duty, devotion, or a desire for healing.

Spiritual desolation that seems like the end of faith is actually a natural, and perhaps inevitable, stop on the journey. Ultimately, it can become a source of hope and strength. The dark night of the soul comes well into the religious voyage; what might prove the undoing of a new believer seems to be a final tempering for the mature religious person in the movement toward God.

Juan de Yepes, as St. John of the Cross was born, began his life of service to others out of necessity. John's father died when he was only seven, and the family was destitute. Juan became an attendant at a hospital for smallpox patients, studied in his spare time, entered a Jesuit college at thirteen, and at the age of twenty-one (in 1563), became a Carmelite monk.

The Carmelites were a mendicant, or beggar, order, but John wished for even greater austerity. Could it be that his lifelong desire for utter simplicity was a way for him to deal with the dark night in his own soul?

For whatever reason, John and his friend Teresa (now known as St. Teresa of Avila) instigated a reform of the Carmelite order, striving tirelessly for absolute poverty and detachment from the world. They even gave up wearing shoes. Their belief was that only by having nothing and desiring nothing could one experience true peace and unity with God. Only then could God's light dawn on the darkness of their souls.

Spiritual struggle

In the dark night of the soul, sometimes the sufferer sees little in which to hope. Sometimes noonday turns into night and the cold dryness of accidie becomes utter despair. As I read the writings of Christian mystics, I doubt whether the dark night of the soul is either uncommon or radically different from our own spiritual struggles.

It's my belief that the pain of every person who is severely depressed, religious or not, is essentially spiritual. Faith and hope are two sides of one coin. The despair of severe depression is a dark night of vanished hope.

However, as Thomas Merton wrote, "Sanctity does not consist in suffering. It is not even directly produced by suffering, for many have suffered and have become devils rather than saints" (Luce 1952, 254). The road of John, Teresa, and Evagrius is not for everyone. Severe self-denial is not a remedy for depression. Suffering may produce endurance, and endurance may produce hope, but suffering is not, in itself, good.

Darkness reframed

In terms of depression, the message that we can take from John of the Cross and Teresa of Avila is that suffering is a mark of the human condition. In the dark night of the soul, one feels the absence of God. I think of the words of Jesus on the cross: "My God, my God, why have you forsaken me?" (Matthew 27:46).

This utter lack of connection must be akin to the lowest periods of depression. How did Evagrius, John, and Teresa find (or help others find) meaning in suffering? *By accepting it.* By recognizing that God could speak to them in their emptiest state.

We agree that suffering is not good in itself. But it exists; you know it all too well. By viewing desolation as an opportunity for spiritual enlightenment and growth, you can reframe it in hopeful, future-leaning terms—if not now, maybe at some time in the future, when melancholy's cloud has passed.

Anfechtungen

Sometimes spiritual desolation is experienced not only as dryness or hopelessness, but also as attack. Martin Luther, the sixteenth-century German monk who became the central catalyst for the Protestant Reformation, used the term *anfechtungen* to express this sense of bombardment.

Martin Luther began life at the dawning of the modern age. Like Evagrius, he was extremely gifted. Luther easily earned his doctorate in a culture that prized rigorous scholarship, and became an esteemed university professor at Wittenberg. (Later, while in protective custody at Wartburg Castle, he translated the New Testament from Greek into German in only eleven days, thus making a significant contribution to standard written German.)

Luther was a devout believer who first sought reform from within the church. But he was not one to back down or compromise his convictions. (My wife commented that she would like to have been Luther's friend, but certainly not his enemy.) When asked by his inquisitors at the Diet of Worms to recant his reformist statements, he refused to budge.

Luther was excommunicated by the church and declared an outlaw; anyone could kill him without fear of punishment. But he had the protection of a German prince (who perhaps had something to do with an Indiana-Jones-like escapade in which Luther was "kidnapped" and held in Wartburg Castle for safekeeping until the situation cooled off). He also had widespread popular support. The Protestant avalanche couldn't be put back; with the growth of the Protestant church in Germany, Luther was able to live out his life in relative safety, using his prodigious gifts as theologian, teacher, translator, writer, musician, pastor, and mediator right up to his death at the age of sixty-five.

Luther also struggled against the noonday demon. Throughout his life, he contended with acute bouts of melancholy. "I myself was offended more than once, and brought to the depth and abyss of despair, so that I wished that I had never been created a man," he wrote (Gritsch & Jenson, 1976 153). Note that he refers to his depression as *offense*. Luther's depression became critical to his understanding of the Christian faith.

Assailed by woes

Like accidie, the term *anfechtungen* has no exact English equivalent. Literally, it means "to be fought at." It interprets the experience of despair, doubt, perplexity, and aloneness as attack. Literally, you are assailed by woes.

Through his struggles, Luther came to believe that this assault of spiritual woes causes us to recognize our need for a loving God. Despair brings us to our knees. From the depths of despair, we learn of our need of God. Luther's own episodes of melancholy helped him recognize his estrangement from God and his need of God's enduring love.

Likewise, our friend Craig came to recognize that he could not force a warm and intimate feeling in his relationship to God. His time of spiritual dryness taught him that his essential human condition is separation from God, and that he can trust in God's promises and presence whether or not he feels a sensation of emotional closeness.

Remedies

What remedies do we have for these spiritual woes? Luther suggested several.

Fight back and stand fast.

Luther counseled that depressed persons must not let despair overtake them, but rather combat depressing thoughts and impulses with all their being: "grit your teeth in the face of your thoughts, and for God's sake be more obstinate, headstrong, and willful than the most stubborn peasant" in fending off this dark valley (Luther Tappert 1955, 90).

Do not let depression rule. Stand up for yourself, fight back, actively wrestle with it. Understanding depression as a spiritual assault may help you view your own role in active terms. Resistance is a natural human response to attack.

In a way, Craig did this by obstinately refusing to let his spiritual dryness take him off course in his devotional life. He stood fast. Eventually, he again felt the warmth of God's love and the emotional depth of that primary relationship.

Keep active.

Fighting back is not enough. We look to Luther's life as well as to his words to learn how he managed to prevail over depression and find periods of happiness. He surrounded himself with people; Luther's hospitality was renowned. He expressed his woes and his hope in music. He campaigned for causes he believed in.

Give service.

Perhaps most important, Luther gave himself in service to others. He worked tirelessly to mediate differences among various warring factions within the Protestant community. As pastor, he cared for his parishioners. Luther is a marvelous example that giving time and energy to the needs of others serves as antidote and safeguard against melancholy. You focus on someone or something other than yourself and thus put your problems in proper perspective.

Seek out joy.

Luther offered yet another recommendation for those assailed by woes: enjoy the fruits of God's creation. Be happy "both inwardly in Christ and outwardly in His gifts and the good things of life. . . . It is for this that He provides His gifts—that we may use them and be glad, and that we may praise, love, and thank God forever and ever" (Ibid, 93).

Go out with friends. Savor what you have. Laugh, tell stories, sing, play games, go to the theater, enjoy a good meal. Turn up the stereo and dance.

Luther had to learn this lesson himself. Concerning his depression, he wrote that he had passed all his former life in "melancholy and depression of spirit, [but] now accept joy and happiness whenever they present themselves—nay, go in search of them" (Bringle 1990, 70–71).

Here Luther emphasized the active response of the one overtaken by despair. *Seek out joy and happiness.* Do not wait for it to happen. Luther recognized that, for all humans, happiness comes in fleeting moments. When happiness occurs (transitory though it may be), relish it. Enjoy it to the fullest.

Luther counseled that one must oppose the torments of despair and depression in every possible way. Live with your depression, as best you can, without allowing it to rule you. Mock it; refuse to take it so seriously that it wears you down until you can't move. Fight back.

Hope in God.

Finally, according to Luther, the most essential response of the religious person who is assailed by woes is a faith-based response. To be depressed is not entirely bad; you recognize that things are not as they should be. Luther believed that hope lies in the Christ who experienced despair and desolation on his journey to the cross. Hear the hope in these lines from a hymn by Luther:

> May God bestow on us his grace,
> With blessings rich provide us,
> And may the brightness of his face
> To life eternal guide us
> That we His saving health may know,
> His gracious will and pleasure. . . . (*Lutheran Book of Worship* 335)

In the midst of seemingly interminable melancholy and loneliness, lacking in hope or any sense of a positive future, Luther would counsel you to trust in the gracious God who promises to be with us and bless us richly. No matter what you *feel*, hold on to the source of hope.

Centuries ago, without benefit of antidepressant drugs or modern psychotherapy, religious people not only coped with despair; they cared for others. But spiritual struggles are not relics of a time long past, nor are they the exclusive territory of mystics and members of religious orders. In fact, they resemble what psychology calls depression. If you have tasted the bitterness of depression, I encourage you to reflect on the ways in which your experience may resemble one of these spiritual struggles.

The next chapter will discuss ways in which you can reevaluate your values and discover meaning and purpose in your life. In essence, these are tasks of spiritual formation. Suffering is not good, but good can come from it. Your spiritual dryness, darkness, or woes can inform and prod you to persevere, to resist, *to act*. Step out in faith toward the warmth and light of a purposeful future.

TAKE ACTION

Take a spiritual approach to healing.

✓ Reflect on the descriptions of spiritual desolation in this chapter and consider how your own experiences are similar/dissimilar. You may want to make notes in your journal or notebook.

✓ Consider how your spiritual life can strengthen you while you are in the process of triumphing over depression.

✓ In your journal or notebook, write down your five most important spiritual strengths or resources (such as prayer, lighting a candle and meditating, spiritual readings, helping others, religious music, etc.).

✓ Consider how you can rely on each of these resources more.

✓ Put at least one of these spiritual strengths or resources into action today.

FOR THE FAMILY

Living with someone who suffers from depression has a spiritual impact.

✓ Read the descriptions of spiritual desolation in this chapter, looking for parallels in your own experience.

✓ List some ways in which your spiritual life can strengthen you while you are in the process of addressing this spiritual struggle.

✓ In your notebook, write your five most important spiritual resources (such as prayer, meditation, scripture, service to others, etc.) and how you can rely on each of them more.

✓ Use at least one these spiritual resources today.

✓ Are there positive ways in which you might share spirituality with your loved one who is depressed?

CHAPTER TWENTY

The Healing Spirit: Values and Purpose Can Defeat Depression

IN THIS CHAPTER YOU WILL:

✓ Discover ways in which values can contribute to health—but also ways in which some of your values may aid and abet your depression.

✓ Examine how values and purpose can give you a sense that life is worthwhile.

✓ Learn the two types of meaning or purpose in life that can benefit the depressed: *ultimate*, referring to your religious belief, your philosophy of life, your core values that drive you and perhaps have driven your family for many generations; and *penultimate*, those highly valued things that give satisfaction, excitement, pleasure and peace, provide *a purpose to each day*, and help us get through the hard parts.

What Do You Value Most in Life?

Do you value accomplishment? Success? Financial security? A beautiful home? A slender figure? Friendship? Good food? Integrity? Hospitality? Being admired by others? Helping others? Nature? Music? Art? Danger? Living painlessly? Freedom to do what you want? Power or authority over others? Politeness? Sexual pleasure? Pleasure, period? Cleanliness? Education? Travel? Humor? Football?

Do you value perfection? Do you hold yourself to an impossibly high standard for every task you undertake? Do you value a rich spiritual life or your relationship with God?

The Importance of Values

Many people assume that our values are either inborn or imparted to us by our parents at such an early age that they are fixed for life. The term itself, *values*, is bandied about in political, social, and religious realms as if everyone knows what it means. We have family values, spiritual values, Christian values, educational values, community values, monetary values. It has become somewhat politically incorrect to question or challenge the values of a particular religious, social, or ethnic group, or sometimes even the values of a particular family or individual.

Actually, our values change as we go through life. Experience, learning, sorrow, and joy shape what we hold to be worthy or unworthy.

Values are subject to scrutiny and assessment. In some cases, community values may outweigh individual values. For example: how should schools handle a student whose family encourages fighting and getting even as a way to deal with conflict? The presenter of a cultural sensitivity workshop once told a group of educators that they shouldn't challenge the parents' values. But, the teachers argued, as representatives of a civilized society, we need to teach children the community value of finding peaceable solutions to conflict.

Values can contribute to health or illness. Some of your values may aid and abet your depression. Unfortunately, many people never intentionally identify what has worth in their lives, and so they make important decisions without really knowing why. They lose focus. Often, they thwart their own prized values because of an impulse, a wish, or a physical or emotional urge.

Assessing your values

Knowing what you value in life will help you control your depression in two important ways. First, you will be in a position to discover which values need building up and which ones are making it hard for you to feel good. Second, you will be able to begin the process of changing unhealthy values into healthy ones that will nourish and build you up in mind, body, and spirit.

Make a list, now. Start with anything you think is worthy or worthwhile, without trying to prioritize the list. Some of your values may be important and others may seem trivial, but put them all down.

Leave wide margins and space between each item for additions and notes. Write for a few minutes, put the notebook down, and come back to it every hour or so until you think you have a pretty complete list of your personal values. Spend a day or two on this exercise if you need to.

Then read over the list critically. Ask questions:

❑   Are these truly my own values, or do I just feel I *should* cherish them?

❑   Is this an important value? Is it essential to my very being?

❑   What values could I probably get along without?

❑   Where did these values come from? Parents? School? Religion? Political beliefs?

❑   Do my values help or hurt me? What impact do they have on others?

❑   Do my values give me a sense of meaning and purpose, a reason for being on this planet? What is that purpose?

❑   Do these values enhance my life and the lives of those around me? Do they benefit the greater good of all people?

❑   Do I actively live by these values?

One way to determine what you hold most dear is to work backward to your values. Make a log of the activities that take up most of your time: work, school, church, golf, watching television, making money, time with your spouse and kids, charitable service, and so forth. Time reveals commitment. What are you committed to? Those are your values. Where does your money go? Those also are your values.

Keep this list going. Throughout a period of time (a week or more), add notations. Write in the margins specific things you have done that support a particular value. Also note things you have done that clash with one or more of your values, or where your own values clash with each other.

You may discover that you can cross some things off the list. These items could go on a "Would Be Nice" list, but they are not your own core values. Almost certainly you will find others to add.

After a week of carefully observing the types of things you actually do and the outcomes from them, you will be ready to consider what values have made it hard for you to live a satisfying life. You will also discover those core values that enhance your life. For example, let's say you prize achievement, excellence, or financial success. What happens if you are laid off and have trouble finding a new job, or discover that others can do your work better than you can? Or perhaps you attach great worth to being an independent, self-reliant sort of person. Does this value make it difficult for you to ask for help when you really need it, to turn to others for comfort, friendship, support, or just laughter and good fun?

Recognizing harmful values

Here are some warning flags to watch for. When carried to extremes, they may contribute to depression.

Perfection.

Nobody's perfect, right? But still you feel compelled to strive for perfection. Either you work yourself into exhaustion in the attempt, or you simply give up and quit trying (rather than accept the possibility of mediocrity or—*GASP!*—failure). Either response can trigger depression or make it worse, whether through exhaustion or ennui, a stifling, world-weary boredom.

Achievement.

Oddly enough (as in the case of perfection), overvaluing achievement may result in lethargy. Things go badly, you have a run of bad luck, your goals are interrupted by one or more crises, and then you feel terrible because you haven't gotten much done. Or you procrastinate, daily castigating yourself for the things you are putting off until tomorrow. Once you reevaluate or reprioritize the importance of achievement, you may discover the value of *being* as well as *doing*.

Choose to sit on the porch and look at the sunset instead of running errands. Decide to pet your dog instead of baking a dozen pies for the marching band fund-raiser. Have a picnic in the park at lunchtime instead of wolfing down a sandwich at your desk.

Demoting (not abolishing) achievement as a cherished value may also lead you to set more realistic and flexible goals. Then, when something goes wrong, you won't feel you've failed. When the crisis passes, you can get back on track without a load of unnecessary guilt dragging you back.

Don't get me wrong; I have made the point throughout this book that staying active and trying to achieve goals on the way to your vision of the future is good and necessary in combating depression. But it's not good to value achievement so highly that you can never meet the mark.

Many other common values, taken to excess, make it difficult to cope with depression. Consider the list below and what might happen if these values (good in themselves) were taken to excess:

❑ Independence

❑ Freedom to do what you want

❑ Pleasure

- ❑ Helping and rescuing

- ❑ Work

- ❑ Good looks

- ❑ Wealth

- ❑ Being with friends

- ❑ Being alone

- ❑ Reading

- ❑ Getting plenty of sleep

- ❑ Devotion to children

- ❑ Feeling safe

- ❑ Being in control

Keep in mind that we do not always act in ways that are congruent with our values; for example, a woman who places a high value on good looks may stay in the house and "let herself go" rather than appear in public as less than the beauty she once was.

If you think about it, nearly any *unbalanced* value can compromise your mental, physical, and spiritual well-being.

Ultimate and Penultimate Purpose

What gets you up in the morning? What gives you a sense that life is worthwhile? What goals are you striving for? What wrongs do you want to right?

I believe that each person needs to have a sense of purpose and meaning in life. This is especially true for those who are depressed. If they have only a hazy sense of purpose, melancholics are likely to view life as more of the relentless suffering they have endured up to the present.

Meaning, purpose, and values always have been attached more to the realms of religion and philosophy, than to psychology. But whatever provides meaning and importance to you is at the heart of how you experience life. Based on what you treasure in life, you decide what you will and will not do.

Values are directly linked to depression. If you have purposes in life that lead you to unhelpful actions, they can cause or deepen depression. Then you need to reassess and make changes in your value and meaning system.

Ultimate purpose in life

There are two types of meaning or purpose in life: ultimate and penultimate. *Ultimate* meaning in life refers to your religious belief, your philosophy of life, your core values that drive you, and perhaps have driven your family for many generations. (Another meaning for *ultimate* is "final.") It's what causes you to work for political causes, to try to right social injustices, to donate a large portion of your family income to a cause. People will sacrifice, sometimes even give their lives, for ultimate values.

Each of us needs to have some force or purpose that helps us make sense of the world around us. This is doubly true for those struggling with depression. If you do not have a clear sense of purpose, it is all too easy to listen to your own depressing thoughts and see no meaning to life. You may come to believe that your distorted, negative worldview is all there is. Why is suicide more prevalent among the deeply depressed? Without a purpose and reason for living, a sense that there can be a better future, taking one's life begins to seem reasonable.

Your purpose in life can help you through hard times. Indeed, if you believe that it is important to endure pain (a natural and inevitable part of every human life) because of your underlying purpose and meaning, then suffering (however unpleasant) fits into your understanding of the journey of life. You view suffering—even emotional suffering such as depression—as part of the bigger picture. Life has purpose, even in the midst of pain.

Penultimate meaning in life

Penultimate purposes in life are those highly valued things and activities that give you satisfaction, excitement, pleasure, and peace. (Another meaning for *penultimate* is "second-to-last.") They excite you, or satisfy you deeply. Playing with your kids after supper, a hobby that consumes you (such as collecting and restoring antique radios—one of my personal penultimate values), cuddling your spouse or grandchildren, religious activities, sports, music, art, auto racing, knitting, baking bread. If you do it as often as circumstances permit, it is probably one of your penultimate values.

Each of us needs to have something to look forward to. Maybe penultimate meaning doesn't shape our total existence, but it provides *a purpose to each day*. It helps us get through the hard parts.

When you first get up in the morning and review what you are going to do that day, what do you look forward to most? What can't you wait to get home to do? Or is it work that motivates you most? For many people who suffer from depression, the answer is "Nothing." If that's your answer, you have a job to do. You need to find something that excites you or provides pleasure, enjoyment, and satisfaction.

That something rarely waltzes in the door and plops down in front of you. Couch potatoes arise! You must explore a number of different choices. Keep your options open. Try several activities. Keep trying until you find something that satisfies you. Each of us needs something to look forward to.

Al had been depressed for many months when his wife dragged him to my office. He was not a willing participant. His answer when I asked him what motivates or enlivens him: "Not a damn thing!" At that, his wife chimed in that all he did was come home and watch TV until he fell asleep in his recliner.

I asked Al what he watched on TV; he said, "Most anything." I pressed the question. He thought for a few seconds and said that he liked to watch the Speed Channel. We talked a little about auto racing. I told him that I used to race stock cars, and Al became more animated. "If you like auto racing," I asked him, "is there something connected with racing that you would like to participate in?" He thought about it, and remembered that he had some acquaintances at work who helped out on a pit crew at a nearby dirt track. He doubted that they needed any help, "but I might ask if they could use a hand. At least it would get me out of the house." His friends were glad to include him. After that, Al had a place to go several nights a week, as well as the excitement of Friday night races.

What if Al had found that they didn't want or need his help, or he didn't like working on a racecar? What if he didn't get along with these guys? He would have had to consider other options—some other hobby, perhaps—or volunteer work, or helping with his son's Little League team, or whatever held even a glimmer of possibility . . . and then *put them into action*.

All people need some form of penultimate meaning for their quality in life, but it is doubly important for those who are susceptible to depression. Riding horses or coaching soccer can help sustain you during down times and provide a degree of a satisfaction while the melancholia is there.

The depressed need to explore both their ultimate and penultimate purpose in life, not only to make sense out of it, but also to help them endure difficult times when they come.

What Do You Value? What Is Your Purpose in Life?

In chapter 19, we saw that Martin Luther's passion for his faith provided ultimate purpose for his life. He also abounded in penultimate meaning. He was a gifted musician and composer; many of his hymns are still sung today. He valued fellowship, good food (and beer!), hospitality, lively conversation, his wife, Kate, and their children.

You can throw inkwells at your demons, as Luther once did. You can rail against melancholy. *But to prevail over your dark mood is to enter fully into life.* It is to move, take action, do something important, give of yourself to others. By aligning your actions with the values you cherish, you will equip yourself to control and defeat depression.

TAKE ACTION

Assess your values.

✓ In the margins of this book, or on a handy piece of paper, jot down the first words that come into you mind when you hear the word "values."

✓ Next, turn back to pages 213–16 in this chapter and follow the directions for assessing your value system.

✓ This exercise will give you a clearer picture of what you cherish, as well as areas where you would do well to adjust your values.

✓ Healthful and authentic values are yours, not someone else's. They help rather than hurt, they provide meaning, and they enhance your life. You live by them.

FOR THE FAMILY

Do not give up on the things you value most.

✓ I urge you to review your ultimate and penultimate values and see that they are not forgotten or ignored while caring for your depressed loved one.

✓ It may be helpful to assess your values, as described on pages 213–16. Do this especially if you suspect that your values have veered off course. You may be going through a necessary course correction, or you may have lost touch with what is *really* important for *you.*

✓ Every morning, review your list. Decide on at least one act you will do that day that supports your highest values. Do not lose yourself or the things you cherish most in life to melancholia's spreading gloom.

CHAPTER TWENTY-ONE

Getting Help

IN THIS CHAPTER YOU WILL:

✓ Acknowledge that sometimes, in addition to the self-help of this book, you may need additional help, and learn that this does not mean you are a failure.
✓ Learn what the signs are that you need to seek help beyond the scope of this book.
✓ Learn how to find a good counselor.
✓ Begin taking an active role in finding and referring your melancholic loved one to community resources, such as physicians, therapists, ministers, marriage and family counselors, financial advisers, attorneys, and employment counselors.

You Can Help Yourself out of Depression

Defeating Depression has been written to help you do just that. Sometimes, though, self-help is not enough. It's beneficial, mind you, just not enough.

This does not mean you are a failure! Seeking outside help is one more way in which you are taking action to put an end to your depression.

Don't give up on what you have learned. Don't stop doing the exercises and action steps that you have already begun. *Add* (don't substitute) the services of a professional who can help you look at your depression from a different perspective. The key is to find the right person to help you. *You* must make that judgment. *You* must decide on courses of action. *You* are in charge of overcoming your depression.

How to Know You Need Help

What are the signs that you need to seek help beyond the scope of this book? Here are some of them:

- ❏ Let's say you have done a number of the exercises suggested in this book and made some changes in your thinking. If depression is still plaguing you, it's appropriate to seek outside help.

- ❏ Do you find yourself contemplating suicide or thinking, "What's the use?" or "People would be better off without me?" *You need professional help right away—and by right away, I mean today.*

- ❏ If you are thinking about suicide but have trouble asking for professional help, tell a neighbor or friend. If all else fails, contact your doctor/minister/therapist or call 911. Do not be embarrassed to do this; the 911 dispatchers and emergency personnel *want you to call.* Nothing shocks them.

- ❏ If depression is disrupting your close relationships (with your spouse or your children, for example), you should consider outside help in addition to the work you're doing from this book.

- ❏ Perhaps you can't bring yourself to do the exercises in this book because you don't have the energy to do much of anything. By all means find someone to help you get started. Don't be shy. (Or go ahead and be shy, but get help anyway.)

- ❏ If your depression is extreme, if it has gone on for years unabated, or if your lows alternate with periods of euphoria (indicating the possibility of bipolar disorder), professional help is in order. Medications may help. Then it is useful to see a psychiatrist or a clinic that has a psychiatrist on staff.

How to Find the Right Helper

Finding a good counselor is not necessarily an easy task. I say this with regret, since you may not have much energy or motivation to undertake this task. But you have to be quite careful about whom you seek for help with your depression. Not all counseling is created equal.

When therapy can make things worse

More than any other aspect of her depression, Hannah hated the fatigue and the weepiness. She didn't feel like doing anything, and often couldn't bring herself to get out of bed in the morning. She broke into tears at the slightest little problem. Broken pencil lead, power failure, dripping faucet, spilled milk. Sometimes she wept for no apparent reason at all.

At her mother's urging, Hannah started seeing a psychotherapist, a respected professional described by her neighbor as caring, accepting, and giving. That sounded good to her.

Each week Hannah poured out her woes to this wonderful counselor. A fresh box of tissues always sat ready by her chair, and she used it. She felt appreciated, understood, heard. Then she went home.

One week led to another. The weeks turned into months, the months into a year. Hannah felt better for fifty minutes a week, but as the weeks and months went by, her depression did not abate. She found it harder and harder to think about anything except her misery. She stopped talking to her children. She stopped cooking. Life didn't seem worth the effort. Hannah began having thoughts of suicide.

How could this be? Many psychotherapists, like Hannah's, will listen to you, talk with you, and comfort you week after week with no end in sight. You may like your therapist very much. You may feel better while you are talking to this person; you may even feel better for the rest of the day.

But if therapy focuses primarily on your problems, your feelings, and your past, and you are not actively involved in taking concrete steps toward goals and solutions—*no matter how good you feel during the session*—it may actually make your depression worse. Not just "no improvement"—*worse*.

Any amount of dwelling on the past, except to capture actions that had positive results before and might work again, rarely brings relief from depression. It can even drive your melancholy lower, darker, and deeper.

Please believe me on this. Liking the therapist (who almost certainly is a good, caring person) and feeling better during the session is seductive and dangerous. There are situations in life when a supportive listening ear is helpful, but depression is *not* necessarily one of them.

> **If you really want a way out of the pit of melancholy, and you find that self-help is not quite enough, it is extremely important to find a therapist who will act as your partner and guide (rather than just your comforter) as you take specific, active steps toward that future.**

An array of cures

Throughout the centuries, helpers have used a great variety of care and counseling methods to offer help for the depressed. Some are still in use today. They include spiritual direction, psychoanalysis, group therapy, long-term therapy, brief counseling, medications, exercise and diet, vitamins, herbal remedies, and more. (We are safely past the eras of leeches, alternating hot and cold baths, and incarceration in chains.)

Some of these approaches have explored the past in the hopes that, once people come to terms with their history, they can function better in the present. Others have tried to change how people think on the assumption that more positive, less cognitively distorted thinking will yield less depression. Still others, supposing that improvement in close relationships will also relieve depression, have specified marriage and family counseling. Those practitioners who accept the physiological basis of depression generally prescribe medications, either alone or in combination with some kind of psychotherapy.

What doesn't work

The U.S. Department of Health and Human Services has monitored research on depression for more than thirty-five years, reviewing various counseling methods and making recommendations concerning their effectiveness. The guidelines prepared for family doctors conclude that: "The efficacy of long-term psychotherapies for the acute phase treatment of major depressive disorder is not known; therefore, these therapies are not recommended for first-line treatment." In plain English: The study did not find benefits of long-term therapy for treating depression and does not recommend it.

What works

The government report instead advocates counseling that is "time-limited, focused on current problems, and aimed at symptom resolution rather than personality change" for the treatment of melancholy (US Vol. II 1993, 4).

The most helpful counseling methods focus on changes in thinking (cognitive therapies), changes in actions (behavioral therapies), and changes in close relationships (interpersonal or marriage and family therapy). The guidelines recommend that therapy be brief, and advise the use of antidepressant medications supplied by a family physician or psychiatrist as well (Ibid., 37).

Are you seeking professional help for yourself or your loved one? You deserve the best help available. You deserve a therapist who will use counseling strategies that work—methods that show superior results in controlled, scientific, up-to-date research studies.

Gathering information

One way to find the right kind of therapist is to get a recommendation from someone who has suffered from depression and overcome it. Talk with friends or family members who have been in therapy to learn from them how their counselor treated them—and in what length of time. Ask specific questions, such as:

- ❏ What helped most?

- ❏ How long did it take?

- ❏ What were you asked to do as a part of the therapy?

- ❏ How do you think differently about the depression?

Ask detailed, pointed questions, not merely "was she any good?" You want the best possible chance at getting better.

If you do not have recommendations from someone who has reason to know, you can start with the *Yellow Pages* or find listings online. You will need a little knowledge to help you wade through all that information.

The two main headings in the *Yellow Pages* will be "Marriage and Family Counselors" and "Psychotherapists." In my city, the longest list is "Psychotherapists" and the second longest is "Marriage and Family Counselors." Psychiatrists are mostly lumped in with "Physicians and Surgeons," although some psychiatrists choose to be listed separately in the "Medical Specialty Guide." There are virtually no listings under "Counselors," "Pastoral Counselors," "Social Workers," or "Licensed Professional Counselors." The list of "Psychologists" is short.

Things to look for

You may find it hard to question a therapist in the quest for someone who can help you with your depression. Your confidence and energy may not seem up to this task. If so, make photocopies of these pages with the list of qualifications and questions. Give the photocopies to a friend, coworker, or family member who will not be afraid to ask tough questions. Let this person do your research for you. Then the two of you can talk—but you alone will make the decision.

Here are some positive catchwords to look for:

- ❏ specialist in depression

- ❏ solution-focused (also called solution-focused brief therapy)

- ❏ behavioral therapy

- ❑ cognitive therapy

- ❑ time-limited therapy

- ❑ rational emotive therapy

- ❑ cognitive-behavioral therapy

- ❑ brief therapy

- ❑ (conjoint) marriage and family therapy

In most large cities, you are likely to find a few expanded listings or display ads in the *Yellow Pages* that give this information (especially the words "solution-focused"). Even if a therapist specializes in counseling for depression, it is important to determine that the counseling is brief in duration and focuses on active solutions rather than analysis.

You can always analyze the causes after you feel better. Right now, it is more important to do those things that will lead you to feeling better.

Duration

First, you or your intermediary needs to call the therapist that you are considering. Ask questions about fees, insurance, and scheduling, to be sure, but also ask about the typical time frame in which the therapist treats depression. You should expect the duration of counseling for depression to be *less than twenty sessions*. Most of the time it will be *less than ten sessions*. If the answer is vague—"It depends on your situation," without any indication that there will be a limit to the time you spend in therapy—try someone else. (Certainly your own situation will determine the exact length of counseling, and your counselor may have been trained to use this phrase for risk-management and ethical reasons. However, if you are a cooperative and willing partner in this enterprise, twenty sessions is a generous outside limit.)

Qualifications

What kind of a degree and qualifications should the therapist have? If you lack a specific recommendation and are looking for a counselor in the *Yellow Pages*, I recommend that you start by calling therapists with an M.C. in counseling, an M.A. in counseling, or a M.S.W., Ph.D. or Ed.D. I suggest that you avoid helpers who primarily do hypnosis, or use the words "psychoanalytic," "long-term," or "psychodynamic." If the depression is very severe and long-term, a psychiatrist is recommended.

If your troubles involve spiritual desolation or other spiritual issues, talk to a clergy person or look under "Pastoral Counselors," if your city's *Yellow Pages* have such a listing. Therapists who advertise themselves as pastoral counselors or Christian counselors can be very helpful, especially if your depression involves issues of meaning or values; but be careful to check the qualifications of these helpers. Do they have the training and supervision to do what they say they can do? As with any other therapist, make sure they are time-limited and solution-focused.

If your problems involve your spouse or family, then look in the *Yellow Pages* under "Marriage and Family Counselors."

This is the one

It won't take long to locate a counselor who treats depression in ways that are similar to the methods presented in this book, whether it's called "solution-focused," "brief," "cognitive," or "behavioral." If possible, it would be good to know whether others in this person's care found relief from their depression. If so, this may be the therapist for you.

Medications

Perhaps you are taking medications for your depression (see chapter 8). This is not necessarily a reason to stay out of counseling. Indeed, antidepressants may give you enough *oomph* or psychic energy to do what you need to do. Once you have that energy, however, it is important that you make some changes in your life to minimize the impact of this episode of depression and to prevent future ones. Therefore, when you choose a therapist, be sure to find someone who will help you focus on things you can do to change your life right away. They may be small steps, but you need to take them.

It is good to remember that in most states only physicians (such as your primary care physician or psychiatrist) can prescribe drugs for mental or emotional difficulties. *Primary care physicians prescribe the vast majority of antidepression medications.* With luck this is someone you already know and trust. Your family doctor can determine if antidepression medication would help.

The first session

During the first session, the counselor will ask you about your symptoms and how long you have had them, and will collect a little background information. She or he will ask you about previous episodes of depression, if any, and the impact of depression on your family and your job. You may find it helpful to write some of this information on a card beforehand and bring it with you.

Counseling Check List

❑ If the first or second session only deals with the past and never gets to goal setting, perhaps you should consider moving on to someone else.

❑ If you are not feeling better and becoming more active as a result of counseling, you need to find another therapist who can help you.

❑ If the counselor doesn't appear to be very compassionate or interested in you, try the next person on your list.

Imagine that you own a vintage car and lack the time or knowledge to work on it. If the first shop you visit doesn't fix the problem, would you keep going back because of their impressive credentials, or because they are so *nice*?

Therapists and auto mechanics are not gods. You are the consumer, and you have every right to keep searching until you find a helper who will focus on solutions to *your* situation.

It is of utmost importance that you participate actively in the process, that you determine how and within what time frame your treatment will take place. If you want the counseling to be over in eight weeks, tell your therapist. Say what you are willing to do to help bring about change at a rapid pace.

How Family Members Can Help

Family members of people suffering from depression need to take an active role in finding and referring their loved one to community resources, such as physicians, therapists, ministers, marriage and family counselors, financial advisors, attorneys, and employment counselors. For example, they might consult with a depressed child's teacher or a food service worker's employer.

Referral always considers the depressed person's mental and emotional states. Some depressed persons will resist seeing anyone at all. It may take some time (and finesse) to nudge them into going to a physician or therapist.

Do you have a loved one who suffers from depression? Do your homework beforehand. When outside help is needed, consider the following suggestions and resources:

❑ Know that the depressed may not accept referral. Merely considering going to a therapist may motivate such people to change. A few, however, only want to complain about their situation rather than move toward a resolution. Still others are so inactive and reclusive that talking to someone is more than they can tolerate.

❑ When uncertain where to refer, talk to friends who have been in therapy—preferably for depression. (Make sure your friend got better within a reasonable period of time!) Or call a local crisis line or an information and referral agency. Dial one of the national depression organizations listed in the box below, or check out the Websites. Explain the situation and get accurate information about appropriate persons or agencies. Call local agencies directly to get answers about waiting lists, fee schedules, and other pertinent information.

❑ Locate several referral sources, if possible, since one may be unavailable when it is needed or your loved one may not click with the first person you suggest.

❑ Make concrete referrals—not "I think you need to see a psychotherapist," but "I'd like to recommend several counselors; Dr. Lind was helpful for my neighbor, and Dr. Goodall has an excellent reputation."

❑ If possible, let the depressed person make the referral call. Suggest dialing the number immediately, or offer a ride to the first appointment.

❑ Always follow up after suggesting a doctor. For example, you might check in the next day to say, "I just want to find out how you are doing today, and to see if you had any problems scheduling a session with Dr. Lind or Dr. Goodall." If you get an excuse, find out other ways you can help. Let the person know that you will check again in a couple of days.

You Are Not Alone

In the midst of dark days, there's no need to go it alone. If you have trouble taking the steps recommended in this book for whatever reason, I urge you to get professional help. If nothing else, you can benefit from the discipline of going to someone every week to report on your progress.

If it is your choice to work with a counselor, do not give up on self-help. No one else can cure your depression! With or without help from a therapist, only you can take action in your own life. Think of yourself as an athlete trying to improve your game; the counselor is your personal coach and cheerleader (not your boss), but you have to do the practice. Your hopeful future is up to you.

INFORMATION AND REFERRAL SOURCES

Consult the following local and national referral sources for help and advice.

✓ Depression Awareness, Recognition, and Treatment (D/ART), (800) 421-4211.

✓ National Institute of Mental Health, (800) 421-4211.

✓ National Mental Health Association, (800) 969-6642.

✓ American Association of Pastoral Counselors (AAPC), (703) 385-6967.

✓ National Depressive and Manic-Depressive Association, (800) 826-3632.

✓ National Foundation for Depressive Illness, (800) 248-4344.

Many other quality sources for information and referral exist both at the local as well as the national level.

WEBSITES

The websites listed below offer helpful links to other sites. BE CAREFUL! There is a lot of junk out there on the Internet. Many commercial sites hawk their own products associated with depression. I have tried to include only legitimate sites that are maintained by associations, responsible individuals, or universities.

✓ **www.veritasmedicine.com/d_index.cfm?did=41&bif=p**
Basic information on depression, medical treatment options, clinical trials of antidepressants, current research, and more. Although primarily advocating a medical approach to treatment, this site has important current information. You can sign up for e-mail updates related to clinical trials and research on depression.

(continued)

✓ **www.depressionalliance.org**
Based in the United Kingdom, the Depression Alliance offers a Website with information on depression, including symptoms of depression; chat rooms and online support activities; a bookshop; and more.

✓ **www.psycom.net/depression.central.html**
A privately-maintained site, Depression Central offers comprehensive information on depression and useful links to other depression-related Websites.

✓ **www.med.nyu.edu/Psych/screens/depres.html**
This online depression screening test sponsored by New York University also includes links to information about depression and referrals for treatment.

✓ **www.depression-screening.org**
In English and Spanish. Maintained by the National Mental Health Association, this site includes online screening, links to information, education, and advocacy opportunities.

✓ **www.depression.org**
The site of the National Foundation for Depressive Illness, this is a basic introduction to depression and its treatments.

✓ **www.walkers.org**
A support network for mood disorders hosted by Walkers in Darkness Inc., this site includes helpful links suggested by members that include information on a variety of mood disorders, including depression.

✓ **www.authentichappiness.org**
This is a Website by Martin Seligman, the author of *Authentic Happiness, Learned Optimism,* and other works on how to be more of an optimist. The site has a number of self-assessment questionnaires users can take.

TAKE ACTION

Let me say it again:

you can help yourself deal with your depression. Sometimes, though, self-help is not enough. It is beneficial, mind you, just not enough. If you find that you need some extra help, it does not mean you are a failure. Seeking outside help is one more way in which *you are taking action* to put an end to the depression. Including the services of a professional who can help you look at your depression from a different perspective may be just what is needed. So, if after three to six weeks of taking action by doing the exercises in this book you find no difference in the depression, make an appointment with a psychotherapist or psychiatrist and get the additional help needed.

FOR THE FAMILY

You can find help for your depressed loved one.

✓ Go back to the "How Family Members Can Help" section in this chapter. Read it again and take its suggestions.

✓ Actively research and locate resources such as physicians, therapists, ministers, marriage and family counselors, financial advisors, attorneys, and employment counselors.

✓ If your loved one is resistant to the idea of getting outside help, keep your list of referral sources handy. Then, when a moment of openness or willingness occurs, you are prepared to make a referral.

✓ If your loved one is nervous or hesitant, offer to drive the car or even to sit in on the first ten minutes of the session. (Do not take over and do the talking, however.)

✓ If the person refuses to consider any form of counseling, seek help for yourself. You could talk to a friend or acquaintance who also has lived with a depressed person, asking what was helpful and what did and did not work.

✓ Talking with a close friend, minister, or therapist can help you make sense of what is happening. It can also protect you from *helper burnout,* a danger for those who are living and caring for a person suffering with depression.

CHAPTER TWENTY-TWO

Hope and Happiness for a Lifetime

IN THIS CHAPTER YOU WILL:

✓ Remember that depression does not have to be a lifestyle; it can be overcome and life can become rich again.
✓ Also remember the Nike motto: "Just do it." If you have not already started, *please,* for yourself and for those around you, *take some of the action steps* outlined in this book—even if they are tiny, seemingly insignificant baby steps that seem pretty easy. Do them now, before you start anything else. Do one in the next minute.

My wife and I like to walk together, anywhere and almost everywhere—through our neighborhood, on mountain trails, deep in the forest, along the streets of foreign cities. But arthritis and old sports injuries took their toll on my knees. I began walking slower and for shorter distances because of the pain. Finally, I faced the facts: I needed double knee surgery.

I'm not a good patient. I don't like getting cut. I'd rather go to the dentist. I'd rather face an audit by the IRS. The only thing I hated more than the prospect of surgery was the prospect of not walking at all. Once the surgery was over, though, I felt grateful.

Next came rehabilitation. While practicing the new-old skill of walking, I reflected that knee surgery and rehabilitation are very much like the way a person overcomes depression. You don't want to go through it. You would rather face the dentist, an IRS auditor, maybe even surgery. But thanks to good research, effective self-help strategies, and recent developments in medications, conquering depression is very possible. Not fun, mind you. Not what you would have chosen when you set out in life, but achievable. You may even learn some new skills while addressing your depression.

There is a way out. Since recovering from knee surgery, I have walked with my wife all over Big Bend National Park (where we had the good fortune to see a mountain lion and two cubs just ahead of us on the trail). We have crested 14,000 feet in the Andes, climbing up through a cloud forest and into the sun. We take long walks in the woods, laughing and plodding along as Skye, our border collie, zigzags through the underbrush at lightning speed after real and imagined squirrels. It is good to be walking again, to be participating in this simple pleasure.

Likewise, there is hope for all of us who struggle with depression from time to time. It isn't necessarily a walk in the park with good knees. Sometimes it's very difficult. But it is doable. There are a host of good methods, tips, and strategies you can use to make it better. To borrow a phrase from 12-step programs, these methods work "if you work them."

What I want to say to you now is an Oprah "You go, girl" and a Nike "Just do it" (even if you're not a girl or an athlete). The low-down pain of depression can be miserable beyond the belief of anyone who hasn't experienced it—but a road leads out of the low place, and you are walking on that road.

You won't arrive by accident. It won't work to sit and wait until you feel better. You have to act, one step by baby step at a time. There will be days when it seems as if you are taking two steps forward and sliding one step (or two, or even three) backward. But even at the end of your worst recovery day you will be a little bit ahead of where you were the day before, because you *did* something. Just getting one of those inevitable bad days out of the way is progress of sorts.

So please, for yourself (and for those around you), take some of the action steps outlined in this book. Perhaps you've already started; if not, choose one or two steps that seem pretty easy. Do them now. Once you succeed with these, add others.

See a physician for a complete physical. There's no shame in talking about your low feelings—but if you can't help feeling embarrassed, write everything down and let the doctor read it.

Think of what you are doing as rehabilitation after surgery. The onslaught of depression was the surgery; now you are attending to the consequences. Rehabilitation takes time. Medications and therapy will help. I went to a good physical therapist after they cut up my knees, and therapy can help your depression as well.

The most important thing is to come up with a plan for your healing. Take the first step. Then keep on going. You don't have to create your action plan out of whole cloth; it's all right to start with the plan suggested in this book (take a look at chapter 14 again). As you succeed at each small step, you can adjust the plan to fit you.

I know you can do it. I urge you to do it. I want you to go walking in Big Bend or the Andes; in other words, I want you to do whatever your heart most desires. Go out and buy your boots. Hit the trail.

Appendix A

The Zung Self-Rating Depression Scale

Name: _____

Age: _____ Sex: _____ Date: _____

Instructions: Read each sentence carefully. For each statement, check the box in the column that best corresponds to how often you have felt that way during the past two weeks. For statements 5 and 7, if you are on a diet, answer as if you were not.

Please check a response for each of the 20 items	None or a little of the time	Some of the time	Good part of the time	Most or all of the time
1 I feel downhearted, blue, and sad	❏	❏	❏	❏
2 Morning is when I feel the best	❏	❏	❏	❏
3 I have crying spells or feel like it	❏	❏	❏	❏
4 I have trouble sleeping through the night	❏	❏	❏	❏
5 I eat as much as I used to	❏	❏	❏	❏
6 I enjoy looking at, talking to, and being with attractive women/men	❏	❏	❏	❏
7 I notice that I am losing weight	❏	❏	❏	❏
8 I have trouble with constipation	❏	❏	❏	❏
9 My heart beats faster than usual	❏	❏	❏	❏
10 I get tired for no reason	❏	❏	❏	❏
11 My mind is as clear as it used to be	❏	❏	❏	❏
12 I find it easy to do the things I used to do	❏	❏	❏	❏
13 I am restless and can't keep still	❏	❏	❏	❏
14 I feel hopeful about the future	❏	❏	❏	❏
15 I am more irritable than usual	❏	❏	❏	❏
16 I find it easy to make decisions	❏	❏	❏	❏
17 I feel that I am useful and needed	❏	❏	❏	❏
18 My life is pretty full	❏	❏	❏	❏
19 I feel that others would be better off if I were dead	❏	❏	❏	❏
20 I still enjoy the things I used to do	❏	❏	❏	❏

How to Use the Self-Rating Depression Scale

The Self-Rating Depression Scale (SDS) comprises a list of twenty items. Each item relates to a specific characteristic of depression. The twenty items together comprehensively delineate the symptoms of depression as they are widely recognized. Opposite the statements are four columns headed: "None or a little of the time," "Some of the time," "Good part of the time," and "Most or all of the time."

For each item on the form, the counselee is asked to check the box according to how it relates to his/her feelings within a specified time period: "during the past two weeks." Although some depressed counselees orally volunteer little information, most will readily cooperate when asked to check the scale if told that this will help the doctor know more about them.

The chart on the facing page will enable you to score the counselee's self-rating depression scale and find out the level of his or her depressive symptomatology.

Find the value of each of the twenty responses by using the number next to the check mark. Total the scores to get the Raw Score. Next, use the conversion table (Raw Score to SDS Index) at the bottom of the page and write the person's SDS Index in the box at the bottom of the last column. The SDS Index is a total indication of "How depressed is the person?" in terms of the operational definition and is expressed as a percentage. Thus, an SDS score of 65 may be interpreted to mean that the person demonstrates 65 percent of the depression measurable by the scale.

By combining results from several studies, the SDS Index can be interpreted as follows:

SDS Index	Equivalent Clinical Global Impressions
Below 50	Within normal range, no psychopathology
50-59	Presence of minimal to mild depression
60-69	Presence of moderate to marked depression
70 and over	Presence of severe to extreme depression

These interpretations are based on data that compare depressed versus nondepressed patients, as well as depressed patients versus normal subjects in the twenty- to sixty-four-year-old range. High scores are not in themselves diagnostic, but indicate the presence of symptoms that may be of clinical significance.

Scoring the Zung Self-Rating Depression Scale

Instructions: Read each sentence carefully. For each statement, check the box in the column that best corresponds to how often you have felt that way during the past two weeks. For statements 5 and 7, if you are on a diet, answer as if you were not.

Please check a response for each of the 20 items	None or a little of the time	Some of the time	Good part of the time	Most or all of the time
1 I feel downhearted, blue, and sad	❏ 1	❏ 2	❏ 3	❏ 4
2 Morning is when I feel the best	❏ 4	❏ 3	❏ 2	❏ 1
3 I have crying spells or feel like it	❏ 1	❏ 2	❏ 3	❏ 4
4 I have trouble sleeping through the night	❏ 1	❏ 2	❏ 3	❏ 4
5 I eat as much as I used to	❏ 4	❏ 3	❏ 2	❏ 1
6 I enjoy looking at, talking to, and being with attractive women/men	❏ 4	❏ 3	❏ 2	❏ 1
7 I notice that I am losing weight	❏ 1	❏ 2	❏ 3	❏ 4
8 I have trouble with constipation	❏ 1	❏ 2	❏ 3	❏ 4
9 My heart beats faster than usual	❏ 1	❏ 2	❏ 3	❏ 4
10 I get tired for no reason	❏ 1	❏ 2	❏ 3	❏ 4
11 My mind is as clear as it used to be	❏ 4	❏ 3	❏ 2	❏ 1
12 I find it easy to do the things I used to do	❏ 4	❏ 3	❏ 2	❏ 1
13 I am restless and can't keep still	❏ 1	❏ 2	❏ 3	❏ 4
14 I feel hopeful about the future	❏ 4	❏ 3	❏ 2	❏ 1
15 I am more irritable than usual	❏ 1	❏ 2	❏ 3	❏ 4
16 I find it easy to make decisions	❏ 4	❏ 3	❏ 2	❏ 1
17 I feel that I am useful and needed	❏ 4	❏ 3	❏ 2	❏ 1
18 My life is pretty full	❏ 4	❏ 3	❏ 2	❏ 1
19 I feel that others would be better off if I were dead	❏ 1	❏ 2	❏ 3	❏ 4
20 I still enjoy the things I used to do	❏ 4	❏ 3	❏ 2	❏ 1

Total (Raw Score)_____

SDS Index _____

Conversion of Raw Scores to SDS Index

Raw Score	SDS Index	Raw Score	SDS Index	Raw Score	SDS Score	Raw Score	SDS Score	Raw Score	SDS Score
20	25	32	40	44	55	56	70	68	85
21	26	33	41	45	56	57	71	69	86
22	28	34	43	46	58	58	73	70	88
23	29	35	44	47	59	59	74	71	89
24	30	36	45	48	60	60	75	72	90
25	31	37	46	49	61	61	76	73	91
26	33	38	48	50	63	62	78	74	92
27	34	39	49	51	64	63	79	75	94
28	35	40	50	52	65	64	80	77	96
29	36	41	51	53	66	65	81	78	98
30	38	42	53	54	68	66	83	79	99
31	39	43	54	55	69	67	84	80	100

Results from several studies have shown that there is usually some depressive symptomatology present in almost all of the psychiatric disorders. Patients may have several diagnoses: headache AND depression, schizophrenia AND depression, diabetes AND depression. Thus, a primary diagnosis other than depression does not eliminate the possibility that the patient is also depressed. If the SDS Index is above 50, the patient may need treatment for the depression in addition to treatment for the primary diagnosis.

Permission was granted to include the Zung Self-Rating Depression Scale in this book. Free copies of the rating scale are available to helpers. Contact:

Eli Lilly and Company
Lilly Corporate Center
U. S. Neuroscience, Constituency Relations
Drop Code 1047
Indianapolis, IN 46285
Fax (317) 277-2387

Appendix B

Suggested Readings and References

Bringle, M. L. 1990. *Despair: Sickness or Sin? Hopelessness and Healing in the Christian Life.* Nashville: Abingdon Press. Beautifully written book that relates depression to religious experiences of despair.

Burns, D. 1980. *Feeling Good: New Mood Therapy.* New York: Morrow. Solid, readable book that focus on changing your thinking which is one of the causes of depression. He also has a handbook with exercises that you can use to help change your negative depressed thinking.

Golant, M. & Golant, S. K. 1996. *What to Do When Someone You Love Is Depressed.* New York: Henry Holt. One of the few books that addresses what family and friends can do when a loved one is depressed.

Hauck, P. 1976. *Overcoming Depression.* Philadelphia: Westminster Press. This book has helped me personally address some of the ways I negatively filter what people say and do and plant the seeds for a depressive episode.

Seligman, M. 2004. *Authentic Happiness.* New York: Free Press. Both of Seligman's recommended books suggest that optimism is learned and suggest ways to be less negative and more optimistic in your thinking.

_____. 1998. *Learned Optimism.* New York: Free Press. Covers some of the same territory as Authentic Happiness. Very good.

Stone, H. W. 1998. *Depression and Hope.* Minneapolis: Fortress Press. In this book I suggest how religious professionals can offer counsel to those who are depressed.

U. S. Department of Health and Human Services. 1993. *Depression in Primary Care: Vol. 1: Detection and Diagnosis.* Also *Depression in Primary Care: Vol. 2: Treatment of Major Depression.* Clinical Practice Guideline No. 5. These two books provide a wealth of information on the causes and treatment of depression by physicians. They can be purchased from the US Government.

Yapko, M. D. 1999. *Hand-Me-Down Blues.* New York: Golden Books. I find all of Michael Yapko's books helpful. This book is written for the family and friends of a person struggling with depression.

_____. 1994. *When Living Hurts: Directives for Treating Depression.* New York: Brunner/Mazel. This Yapko book, although written primarily for clinicians, covers a variety of ways to treat depression.

References

American Psychiatric Association (APA). 1993. "Practice Guidelines for Major Depressive Disorder in Adults." *American Journal of Psychiatry* 150: 4, 1-26.

American Psychiatric Association (APA). 1994. *Diagnostic and Statistical Manual of Mental Disorders*, 4th ed., rev. Washington, DC: American Psychiatric Association.

Agatston, A. 2003. *The South Beach Diet*. New York: Rodale Press.

Antonuccio, D. O., W. G. Danton, and G. Y. DeNelsky. 1995. "Psychotherapy Versus Medication for Depression: Challenging the Conventional Wisdom With Data." *Professional Psychology: Research and Practice* 26: 6, 574-585.

Assagioli, R. 1965. *Psychosythesis*. New York: Hobbs, Dorman & Company.

Bandler, R., and J. Grinder, 1979. *Frogs Into Princes*. Moab, Utah: People Press.

Bateson, G. 1987. *Steps to an Ecology of Mind*. Northvale, NJ: Jason Aronson.

Beach, S. R. H., and G. M. Nelson. 1990. "Pursuing Research on Major Psychopathology from a Contextual Perspective: The Example of Depression and Marital Discord." In *Family Research*, Vol. 2. Edited by G. Brody, and I. E. Sigel. Hillsdale: Lawrence Erlbaum, 227-260.

_____, E. E. Sandeen, & K. D. O'Leary. 1990. "A Randomized Clinical Trial of Inpatient Family Intervention: V. Results for Affective Disorders." *Journal of Affective Disorder*, Vol. 18, 17-28.

Beck, A. T. 1967. *Depression*. New York: Harper and Row.

_____, G. Brown, R. A. Steer, J. I. Eidelson, and J. H. Riskind. 1979. *Cognitive Therapy of Depression*. New York: Guilford Press

Breggin, P. and G. R. Breggin. 1994. *Talking Back to Prozac*. New York, NY: St. Martin's Press.

Bringle, M. L. 1990. *Despair: Sickness or Sin? Hopelessness and Healing in the Christian Life*. Nashville: Abingdon Press.

_____. 1996. "Soul-Dye and Salt: Integrating Spiritual and Medical Understandings of Depression." *Journal of Pastoral Care* 40: 329-340.

Brown, G. W., and T. O. Harris. 1978. *Social Origins of Depression: A Study of Psychiatric Disorder in Women*. New York: Free Press.

Burns, D. 1980. *Feeling Good: New Mood Therapy*. New York: Morrow.

Casey, M. 1995. *Sacred Reading*. Liguori, MO: Triumph Books.

Cowley, G. 1994. "The Culture of Prozac." *Newsweek* Feb.7, 41-42.

Dayringer, R. 1995. *Dealing with Depression*. New York: The Haworth Press.

Diener, E., R. Emmons, and S. Griffin. 1985. "The Satisfaction with Life Scale." *Journal of Personality Assessment* 49: 71-75.

de Shazer, S. 1985. *Keys To Solution In Brief Therapy*. New York: W. W. Norton.

_____. 1988. *Clues: Investigating Solutions in Brief Therapy*. New York: W. W. Norton.

DeBattista, C., and A. Schatzberg. 1995. "Somatic Therapy." In *Treating Depression*. Edited by I. Glick. San Francisco: Jossey-Bass, 153-181.

DeRosis, H. and V. Pellegrina. 1976. *The Book of Hope*. New York: McMillan.

Ellis, A. & R. Harper. 1976. *A New Guide to Rational Living*. North Hollywood: Wilshire Press.

Farberow, N., S. Heilig, and R. Litman. 1968. *Techniques in Crisis Intervention: A Training Manual*. Los Angeles: Suicide Prevention Center, Inc.

Fawcett, J. 1993. "The Morbidity and Mortality of Clinical Depression." *International Clinical Psychopharmacology* 8: 217-220.

Field, T., B. Healy, S. Goldstein, and M. Guthertz. 1990." Behavior-State Matching and Synchrony in Mother-Infant Interactions of Non-depressed Versus Depressed Dyads." *Developmental Psychology* 26: 7-14.

Frankl, V. 1963. *Man's Search for Meaning*. New York: Washington Square Press.

Gordon, D., D. Burge, C. Hammen, C. Adrian, C. Jaenicke, and D. Hiroto. 1989. "Observations of Interactions of Depressed Women with Their Children." *American Journal of Psychiatry* 146: 50-55.

Gove, W. R., M. Hughes, and C. B. Style. 1983. "Does Marriage Have Positive Effects on the Psychological Well-Being of an Individual?" *Journal of Health and Social Behavior* 24: 122-131.

Gritsch, E. and R. Jenson. 1976. *Lutheranism: The Theological Movement and Its Confessional Writings*. Philadelphia: Fortress Press.

Hamilton, M. 1969. "A Rating Scale for Depression." *Journal of Neurology, Neurosurgery, and Psychiatry* 23: 56-62.

Hassler, J. 1985. *A Green Journey*. New York: Ballatine Books.

Hauck, P. 1976. *Overcoming Depression*. Philadelphia: Westminster Press.

Hollon, S., R. DeRubeis, and M. Seligman. 1992. "Cognitive Therapy and the Prevention of Depression." *Applied and Preventive Psychology* 1: 89-95.

Ilfeld: F. W. 1977. "Current Social Stressors and Symptoms of Depression." *American Journal of Psychiatry* 134: 161-166.

Kabot-Zinn, J. 2001. Full Catastrophe Living. London: Piatkus Books.

Kazdin, A. E. 1989. "Childhood Depression." *In Treatment of Childhood Disorders*. Edited by E. J. Mash, and R. A. Barkley. New York: Guilford Press, 495-511.

Keitner, G. I., I. W. Miller, N. B. Epstein, and D. S. Bishop, 1986. "The Functioning in Families of Patients with Major Depression." *International Journal of Family Psychiatry* 7:11-16.

Loftus, J. A. 1983. *Some Relationships Between Spiritual Desolation as Defined in the First Week of the Spiritual Exercises of Ignatius Loyola and Clinical Depression as Presented in Contemporary Psychological Theories*. Doctoral dissertation, Boston University Graduate School. Boston.

Lowen, Alexander. 1973. *Depression and the Body*. Baltimore: Penguin.

Luce, C. B., ed. 1952. *Saints for Now*. New York: Sheed & Ward 1952

Luther, M. 1955. *Letters of Spiritual Counsel*. Edited and translated by T. Tappert. Philadelphia: Westminster Press.

Madanes, C. 1984. *Behind the One-Way Mirror*. San Francisco: Jossey-Bass.

Neuger, C. C. 1991. "Women's Depression: Lives at Risk" in *Women in Travail and Transition*. Edited by M. Glaz and J. S. Moessner, Minneapolis: Fortress Press, 146-161.

Palmer, P. 1995. "Action and Insight: An Interview with Parker Palmer." *The Christian Century*, (March 22-29), 326-329.

Potter, W., M. Rudorfer, and H. Manji. 1991. "The Pharmacologic Treatment of Depression." *The New England Journal of Medicine*. Vol 325: 9 Aug. 29, 633-642.

Prince, S. and N. Jacobson. 1995. "A Review and Evaluation of Marital and Family Therapies for Affective Disorders." *Journal of Marital and Family Therapy* 21: 377-401.

Radke-Yarrow, M., E. Nottlemann, B. Belmont, and J. D. Welsh. 1993. "Affective Interactions of Depressed and Non-depressed Mothers." *Journal of Abnormal Child Psychology* 21: 683-695.

Raskin, A., J. Schulterbrandt, N. Reatig, & J. J. McKeon.1970. "Differential Response to Chlorpromazine, Imipramine, and Placebo: A Study of Sub-Groups of Hospitalized Depressed Patients." *Archives of General Psychiatry* 23 (2): 164-173.

Regier, D., W. E. Narron, D.S. Rae, R. W. Manderscheid, B. Z. Locke, & F. K. Goodwin. 1993. "The de facto US Mental and Addictive Disorders Service System." Archives of General Psychiatry 50: 85-94.

Seligman, M. 1973. "Fall into Helplessness." *PsychologyToday* 7: 43-48.

_____. 1974. "Depression and Learned Helplessness." In *The Psychology of Depression: Contemporary Theory and Research*. Edited by R. Friedman and M. Katz. Washington, D. C.: Winston, 144-161.

_____. 1983. "Learned Helplessness." In *Depression: Concepts, Controversies, and Some New Facts*, second edition. Hillsdale, N. J.: Erlbaum, 64-72.

Stone, H. W. 2008. *Crisis Counseling*, third edition, revised. Minneapolis: Fortress Press.

_____. 1994. *Brief Pastoral Counseling*. Minneapolis: Fortress Press.

_____. 1998. *Depression and Hope*. Minneapolis: Fortress Press.

_____, and J. Duke. 2006. *How to Think Theologically*. Minneapolis: Fortress Press.

Tellenbach, H. 1980. *Melancholy*. Pittsburgh: Duquesne University Press.

U. S. Department of Health and Human Services. 1993. *Depression in Primary Care: Vol. 1: Detection and Diagnosis*. Clinical Practice Guideline No. 5.

_____. 1993. *Depression in Primary Care: Vol. 2: Treatment of Major Depression*. Clinical Practice Guideline No. 5.

Weiner-Davis, M., S. de Shazer, and W. J. Gingerich. 1987. "Building on Pretreatment Changes to Construct the Therapeutic Solution: An Exploratory Study." *Journal of Marital and Family Therapy*, 13 (4), 359-363.

Weissman, M. M. 1987. "Advances in Psychiatric Epidemiology: Rates and Risks for Major Depression." *American Journal of Public Health*. 77: 445-451.

_____, and G. L. Klerman. 1985. "Sex Differences in the Epidemiology of Depression." *Archives of General Psychiatry*, 34, 98-111.

Wenzel, S. 1967. *The Sin of Sloth: Acedia in Medieval Thought and Literature*. Chapel Hill, N. C.: University of North Carolina Press.

Wilson, T. D. 2002. *Stranger to Ourselves: Discovering the Adaptive Unconscious*. Belknap Press.

Yapko, M. D. 1992. *Free Yourself from Depression*. Emmaus, Pa: Rodale Press.

_____. 1999. *Hand-Me-Down Blues*. New York: Golden Books.

_____. 1994. *When Living Hurts: Directives for Treating Depression*. New York: Brunner/ Mazel.

_____. September 14, 1996 speech. "Listening to Prozac...But Talking to Clients: Brief Methods for Treating Depression," Our Lady of the Lake University, San Antonio, Texas.

Zung, W. W. 1965. "A Self-Rating Depression Scale." *Archives of General Psychiatry* 23: 63-70.

Index

Accedie, 204-207

Adolescents, 187, 189-90

Anfechtungen, 207-209

Antidepressant medication, 42, 67, 87-95, 223, 226

Behavioral intervention, 135-68, 223

Bipolar disorder, 23, 92, 221

Characteristics of depression, 28-39, 60

Children, 37, 65, 172-74, 178, 187-90

Cognitions, 98

Cognitive restructuring, 103-104

Concrete thinking, 101-102

Control, 110-15, 124-25, 150-52, 180

Dark night of the soul, 95, 205-206

Dis-identification, 121-22

Either/or thinking, 100-101, 104, 154

Emotional reasoning, 102-104

Evagrius, 203-207

Exceptions, 57, 103, 114, 117-19, 133-34, 141, 160, 183

Exercise, 77, 79, 83, 162, 167

Future question, 137-39, 141

Gender differences, 38

Goals, 53, 120, 131, 137, 140-43, 148, 184-85, 215-16

Grief, 13, 22-23, 45

Hope, 8, 33, 51-60, 99, 119-21, 140, 178-79, 195, 205-209, 233-34

Inner critic, 103, 105, 129-31

Interpersonal, 4, 8, 13, 31, 35-37, 60, 95, 159, 171-72, 194, 199-200, 223

Luther, Martin, 22, 207-209, 218-19

Miracle question, 137-39

Major depression, 4-5, 13, 16-17, 23-24, 47, 90, 92

Marriage, 35-37, 173-74, 178-85, 197, 223-27

Marriage counseling, 198-200, 223-27

Misplaced concreteness, 102

Monoamine oxidose inhibitors (MAOI), 88-91

Neurotransmitter, 66, 88-92

Obsessive thoughts, 84, 91, 110-15

Overgeneralization, 100

Personalization, 100

Physiology, 24-25, 64, 73

Quick action plan, 161-63

Referral, 94, 189, 220-32

Reframing, 56-58, 177

Selective serotonin re-uptake inhibitors (SSRI), 87-92

Sleep disturbance, 16, 23, 32, 46, 65, 70, 75-78, 162, 167-68, 189

Spiritual desolation, 39, 203-207

Spiritual direction, 226

Strengths, 26, 56, 110, 114, 136-37, 142, 160, 177, 183-84, 210

Suicide, 9, 17-18, 34, 88, 184, 189-90, 194-201, 217, 221-22

Thought stopping, 112-13

Tricyclic medications, 90-92

Worry time, 110-11

Zung Self-Rating Scale, 16, 235-38

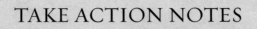

TAKE ACTION NOTES

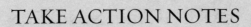

TAKE ACTION NOTES

TAKE ACTION NOTES

TAKE ACTION NOTES